D1433912

The Education of a
British-Protected Child

Also by Chinua Achebe

Anthills of the Savannah
The Sacrificial Egg and Other Stories
Things Fall Apart
No Longer at Ease
Chike and the River
A Man of the People
Arrow of God
Girls at War and Other Stories
Beware Soul Brother
Morning Yet on Creation Day
The Trouble with Nigeria
The Flute
The Drum
Home and Exile
Hopes and Impediments
How the Leopard Got His Claws (with John Iroaganachi)
Winds of Change: Modern Short Stories from Black Africa (coeditor)
African Short Stories (editor, with C. L. Innes)
Another Africa (with Robert Lyons)

The Education of a
British-Protected Child

CHINUA ACHEBE

The Education of a British-Protected Child

ESSAYS

PENGUIN CLASSICS
an imprint of
PENGUIN BOOKS

PENGUIN CLASSICS

Published by the Penguin Group
Penguin Books Ltd, 80 Strand, London WC2R ORL, England
Penguin Group (USA) Inc., 375 Hudson Street, New York, New York 10014, USA
Penguin Group (Canada), 90 Eglinton Avenue East, Suite 700, Toronto, Ontario, Canada M4P 2Y3
(a division of Pearson Penguin Canada Inc.)
Penguin Ireland, 25 St Stephen's Green, Dublin 2, Ireland (a division of Penguin Books Ltd)
Penguin Group (Australia), 250 Camberwell Road,
Camberwell, Victoria 3124, Australia (a division of Pearson Australia Group Pty Ltd)
Penguin Books India Pvt Ltd, 11 Community Centre,
Panchsheel Park, New Delhi – 110 017, India
Penguin Group (NZ), 67 Apollo Drive, Rosedale, North Shore 0632, New Zealand
(a division of Pearson New Zealand Ltd)
Penguin Books (South Africa) (Pty) Ltd, 24 Sturdee Avenue,
Rosebank, Johannesburg 2196, South Africa

Penguin Books Ltd, Registered Offices: 80 Strand, London WC2R ORL, England

www.penguin.com

First published in the United States of America by Alfred A. Knopf, a division of Random House, Inc., New York 2009
First published in Great Britain by Penguin Classics 2010

1

Copyright © Chinua Achebe, 2009

The moral right of the author has been asserted

Printed in Great Britain by Clays Ltd, St Ives plc

A CIP catalogue record for this book is available from the British Library

978–1–846–14259–8

www.greenpenguin.co.uk

For Charles P. Stevenson, Jr.

Contents

Contents

Preface

In 2008, my first novel, *Things Fall Apart*, celebrated its fiftieth anniversary. Many people in different parts of the world joined in the festivities; it was quite a season. There were big intellectual conventions and small street-side performances. The people of my Nigerian hometown, Ogidi—which we still fondly call a village—went completely out of their way in originality and sheer audacity. They checked their stock, and took an ancient festival called Nwafor and turned it into the celebration of a book.

Was this reinvention of our regional festival a challenge to our ancestors and gods? In such dangerous situations, Ogidi people draw upon their wisdom and step carefully. Of all the festivities available to them, they chose Nwafor, a secular celebration dedicated to play and fun, feasting and fellowship; they avoided feuding deities. It was this joyful annual festival that Ogidi people decided to offer to *Things Fall Apart*, a book celebrating the immemorial customs of Ogidi for the first time in written fiction!

As the festival got underway, the old men and women of the town were perhaps puzzled by the events swirling around them, but not so their children, who were ready to embrace a more modern approach. I am told that a very talented actor—who had once played the role of Okonkwo with great success in a theatrical interpretation of *Things Fall Apart* performed in the state capital—was brought to the Ogidi town hall. There, his every step was cheered by the villagers. They could accept and recognize the unusual events going on around them, both about a book and everything else we now call our history.

During these celebrations, I thought also about this new book, a collection of essays that spans my career as a writer. I had high hopes for it. I wanted very much to shine the torch of variety and of difference on the experiences my life has served up to me, illuminating what it is that unites my writing and my personal life. I knew this would be hard to do; the book's success would depend on what seamless effect I might contrive to tie these experiences together. This book would have to deal with real individual people, times, and topics. But there was no list that I was trying to complete, no group that I was making it my business to study from. This book would be personal and eclectic, therefore one could not look to it with scholarly intentions to learn about me completely.

I began to pull together the various pieces. The essay called "My Daughters" took its place without a fuss. I continued, working on other subjects, until my editor read the collection and asked me, "What about the boys?" I knew immediately that the next question would be: "Where is your wife?" and that my entire scheme for this collection—which passed over certain aspects of my life—was untenable. Would I also leave out the motor accident that, in 1990, cost me the use of my legs? What would I tell about the accident—except that my son and I were in the backseat and that it was he who, unable to roll the car away from me, rushed back to the road and shouted my name so that every car stopped and they took me to a hospital. . . . If my son hadn't been there it would have been a different story.

My wife, Christie, was teaching her favorite counseling class to graduate students at the University of Nigeria when they brought her the news of my accident. She put her professional life on hold then and there; and now. It was Christie and our two girls—Chinelo and Nwando—and two boys—Ikechukwu and Chidi—who saw me through. Would I—could I—write about all of this? No, I knew this book would have gaps and deletions as topics and essays moved naturally from one to the next.

As I completed the book, an invitation I had earlier received from the Library of Congress in Washington, D.C., served as an opportunity to bring together the events from my past with some thoughts of the future. The library had asked me to join them in celebrating the anniversary of *Things Fall Apart*, as well as my seventy-eighth birthday. When this occasion arrived, I was very well received by the staff of the library. They couldn't stop telling me how proud they were that I was actually present. The date was November 3, 2008.

I had a full house. An incredible drummer from Cameroon held us in his spell. I read my poems and signed copies of my books. Then, to a great burst of applause, I watched a huge birthday cake coming up the ramp slowly towards me. All I could say by way of speech was: "Is this what you normally do?" I don't know what answer I expected. But I remember a most extraordinary comment made to me earlier that day by an African-American lady. She had thanked me once again for my visit and added, with an element of both bargain and folklore: "And tomorrow we shall elect an African president *for you.*"

It is likely that in years to come folks will be asking their fellows what they were doing when Barack Obama was elected president. I hope we shall not be asking where we were or what we were doing but what the news did to us.

Chinua Achebe
Annandale-on-Hudson, New York
2009

*The Education of a
British-Protected Child*

The Education of a British-Protected Child

The title I have chosen for these reflections may not be immediately clear to everybody and, although already rather long, may call for a little explanation or elaboration from me. But before I get to that, I want to deal with something which gives me even more urgent cause for worry—its content.

I hope my readers are not expecting to encounter the work of a scholar. I had to remind myself, when I was invited to give this address, that if they think you are a scholar, it must mean you are a scholar, of sorts. I say this "up front," as Americans would put it, to establish the truth quite early and quite clearly in case somehow a mistake has been made.

Though I would much rather have a successful performance than the satisfaction of being exonerated in failure, I

In its original form, this essay was delivered as the Ashby Lecture at Cambridge University, January 22, 1993. Eric Ashby, for whom the Ashby Lecture series is named, was master of Clare College at the university from 1959 to 1967. The lectures' broad theme is that of human values.

cannot help adding that failure, sad as it would be, might also reveal the workings of poetic justice, because I missed the opportunity of becoming a clear-cut scholar forty years ago when Trinity College, Cambridge, turned down my application to study there after I took my first degree at the new University College, Ibadan. My teacher and sponsor from Ibadan had been a Cambridge man himself—one James Welch, about whom I shall say a few more words later. Anyhow, I stayed home then, and became a novelist. The only significant "if" of that personal history is that you, ladies and gentlemen, would be reading a scholarly essay today rather than an impressionistic story of a boy's growing up in British colonial Nigeria.

As you can see already, nothing has the capacity to sprout more readily or flourish more luxuriantly in the soil of colonial discourse than mutual recrimination. If I become a writer instead of a scholar, someone must take the rap. But even in such a rough house, masked ancestral spirits are respected and accorded immunity from abuse.

In 1957, three years after my failed Cambridge application, I had my first opportunity to travel out of Nigeria to study briefly at the BBC Staff School in London. For the first time I needed and obtained a passport, and saw myself defined therein as a "British Protected Person." Somehow the matter had never come up before! I had to wait three years more for Nigeria's independence in 1960 to end that rather arbitrary protection.

I hope nobody is dying to hear all over again the pros and cons of colonial rule. You would get *only* cons from me, anyway. So I want to indulge in a luxury which the contemporary culture of our world rarely allows: a view of events from neither the foreground nor the background, but the *middle* ground.

That middle ground is, of course, the least admired of the three. It lacks luster; it is undramatic, unspectacular. And yet my traditional Igbo culture, which at the hour of her defeat had ostensibly abandoned me in a basket of reeds in the waters of the Nile, but somehow kept anxious watch from concealment, ultimately insinuating herself into the service of Pharaoh's daughter to nurse me in the alien palace; yes, that very culture taught me a children's rhyme which celebrates the middle ground as most fortunate:

Obu-uzo anya na-afu mmo
Ono-na-etiti ololo nwa
Okpe-azu aka iko

The front one, whose eye encounters spirits
The middle one, the dandy child of fortune
The rear one of twisted fingers.

Why do the Igbo call the middle ground lucky? What does this place hold that makes it so desirable? Or, rather, what misfortune does it fence out? The answer is, I think, Fanaticism. The One Way, One Truth, One Life menace. The Terror that lives completely alone. So alone that the Igbo call it *Ajo-ife-na-onu-oto:* Bad Thing and Bare Neck. Imagine, if you can, this thing so alone, so singularly horrendous, that it does not even have the company of a necklace on its neck. The preference of the Igbo is thus not singularity but duality. Wherever Something Stands, Something Else Will Stand Beside It.

The middle ground is neither the origin of things nor the last things; it is aware of a future to head into and a past to fall back on; it is the home of doubt and indecision, of suspension of disbelief, of make-believe, of playfulness, of the unpredictable, of irony. Let me give you a thumbnail sketch of the Igbo people.

When the Igbo encounter human conflict, their first impulse is not to determine who is right but quickly to restore harmony. In my hometown, Ogidi, we have a saying, *Ikpe Ogidi adi-ama ofu onye:* The judgment of Ogidi does not go against one side. We are social managers rather than legal draftsmen. Our workplace is not a neat tabletop but a messy workshop. In a great compound, there are wise people as well as foolish ones, and nobody is scandalized by that.

The Igbo are not starry-eyed about the world. Their poetry does not celebrate romantic love. They have a proverb, which my wife detests, in which a woman is supposed to say that she does not insist that she be loved by her husband as long as he puts out yams for lunch every afternoon. What a drab outlook for the woman! But wait, how does the man fare? An old villager once told me (not in a proverb but from real life): "My favorite soup is egusi. So I order my wife never to give me egusi soup in this house. And so she makes egusi every evening!" This is then the picture: The woman forgoes love for lunch; the man tells a lie for his supper!

Marriage is tough; it is bigger than any man or woman. So

the Igbo do not ask you to meet it head-on with a placard, nor do they ask you to turn around and run away. They ask you to find a way to cope. Cowardice? You don't know the Igbo.

Colonial rule was stronger than any marriage. The Igbo fought it in the battlefield and lost. They put every roadblock in its way and lost again. Sometimes I am asked by people who read novels as if novels were history books, what made the conversion of my people to Christianity in *Things Fall Apart* so easy.

Easy? I can tell you that it was *not* easy, neither in history nor in fiction. But a novel cannot replicate historical duration; it has to be greatly compressed. In actual fact, Christianity did not sweep through Igboland like wildfire. One illustration will suffice. The first missionaries came to the Niger River town of Onitsha in 1857. From that beachhead they finally reached my town, Ogidi, in 1892. Now, the distance from Onitsha to Ogidi is only seven miles. Seven miles in thirty-five years: that is, one mile every five years. That is no whirlwind.

I must keep my promise not to give a discourse on colonialism. But I will state simply my fundamental objection to colonial rule.

In my view, it is a gross crime for anyone to impose himself on another, to seize his land and his history, and then to compound this by making out that the victim is some kind of ward or minor requiring protection. It is too disingenuous. Even the aggressor seems to know this, which is why he will sometimes camouflage his brigandage with such brazen hypocrisy.

In the closing years of the nineteenth century, King Leopold II of the Belgians, whose activity in the Congo became a byword for colonial notoriety, was yet able to utter these words with a straight face:

> I am pleased to think that our agents, nearly all of whom are volunteers drawn from the ranks of the Belgian Army, have always present in their minds a strong sense of the career in which they are engaged, and are animated with a pure feeling of patriotism; not sparing their own blood, they will the more spare the blood of the natives, who will see in them the all powerful *protectors* of their lives and their property, benevolent teachers of whom they have so great a need.[1]

It would be downright silly to suggest a parallel between British colonial rule in Nigeria and the scandalous activity of His Serene Majesty Leopold II in the Congo. And yet we cannot ignore the basic assumption of all European powers that participated in the Scramble for Africa. Just as all of Europe had contributed to the making of the dreadful character Mr. Kurtz, in Conrad's *Heart of Darkness,* so had all of Europe collaborated in creating the Africa that Kurtz would set out to deliver and that he would merely subject to obscene terror.

The grandiose words of King Leopold II may remind us that the colonizer was also wounded by the system he had created. He may not have lost land and freedom, like his colonized victim, but he paid a number of seemingly small prices, like the loss of a sense of the ridiculous, a sense of proportion, a sense of humor. Do you think Leopold II would have been capable of saying to himself: "Knock it off, chum; this is sheer humbug. You know the reason your agents are over there killing and maiming is that your treasury needs the revenue from rubber and ivory"? Admission of guilt does not necessarily absolve the offender, but it may at least shorten the recital and reliving of painful evidence.

What about the victim? Dispossession is, of course, no laughing matter, no occasion for humor. And yet the amazing thing is that the dispossessed will often turn his powerlessness to good account and laugh, and thereby lift himself out of desolation and despair. And save his humanity by the skin of his teeth, for humor is quintessentially human!

My mother, after she was betrothed to my evangelist father at the turn of the twentieth century, was sent to the newly founded St. Monica's Girls' School in our district, the first of its kind in Igboland. As a special favor, she went to live with the principal, Miss Edith Ashley Warner, and her small band of English teachers, and performed domestic chores in return for her education and keep. The daughter of a village ironsmith, she found her new life strange, exciting, and sometimes frightening. Her most terrifying early experience, the discovery one night in a bowl of water her mistress's dentures or, in my mother's words, her "entire jaw."

When I was growing up, thirty and more years later, the picture of Miss Warner still hung on our wall. She was actually quite good-looking, and her jaw seemed all right in the photograph. A "complete lady," in Amos Tutuola's word.

One evening she told my mother to eat the food in the dish and afterwards to wash it carefully. She was apparently learning the Igbo language and used it on this occasion. She said, *"Awakwana afele,"* which should mean "Don't break the plate," except that Igbo verbs are sometimes quite tricky. My mother, unable to contain her amusement, gave way to a barely suppressed giggle, which proved to be a great mistake. The Victorian lady was not amused. She picked up a huge stick and walloped her good and proper. Later on she called her and gave her a stern lecture on good manners: "If I speak your language badly, you should tell me the right way. It is wrong to laugh at me," or words to that effect.

My mother told that story many times in my hearing and each time we would all laugh all over again, because *"Awakwana afele"* is quite hilarious baby talk.

By the time it was my turn to go to primary school, in 1936, missionary teachers like Miss Warner were no longer around. Education at that level was completely in the hands of native teachers, but the legacy of the unspared rod remained, with just one small amendment. You were walloped not for laughing when a mistake was made, but for making it.

The Chinese did not invent wall posters for cultural education. My father did. Beside the picture of Miss Warner was a framed motto of St. Monica's School in blue letters. It said "Speak true, Live pure, Right wrong, Follow the king."

As I began to learn my first English words at school, I would naturally test my ability on various wall hangings in our home. I remember the difficulty I had figuring out "Right wrong." I kept wondering which it was—right or wrong! I am certain that even the earnest Miss Warner would have smiled at the problem I was having with English nouns and verbs.

My father filled our walls with a variety of educational material. There were Church Missionary Society yearly almanacs, with pictures of bishops and other dignitaries. But the most interesting hangings were the large paste-ups which my father created himself. He had one of the village carpenters make him large but light frames of soft white wood onto which he then gummed brown or black paper backing. On this paper he pasted colored and glossy pictures and illustrations of all kinds from old magazines. I remember a most impressive picture of King George V in red and gold, wearing a sword. There was also a funny-looking little man with an enormous stride. He was called Johnnie Walker. He was born in 1820, according to the picture, and was still going strong. When I learnt many years later that this extraordinary fellow was only an advertisement for Scottish whiskey, I felt a great sense of personal loss. There was an advertisement from the Nigerian Railways in which the big "N" and "R" served also for "National Route." That also gave me some trouble, as I recall reading it as "Nigerian National Railway Route," which made some kind of sense too!

So my education went from the walls of our home in a haphazard fashion through the village to St. Philip's C.M.S. Central School and back again.

It was sheer effrontery, hinting at any kind of comparison between my puny story and the story of Moses at the beginning of this account. It was like the glowworm comparing itself to the full moon. I do apologize. I was carried away. But the village of Ogidi did keep surreptitious watch over me through the exile of Christianity. My river, though, was not the Nile but the Niger. Indeed, our official title was the Diocese on the Niger. Not *of* the Niger but *on*. Our bishop was Bishop on the Niger.

The village of Ogidi was only part Christianized when I was growing up and still provided its traditional sights and sounds from which I—a Christian child—was technically excluded, an exclusion making them all the more compelling. Like all children I looked forward to the Nwafor Festival, the major holiday of the traditional year, during which ancestral masquerades of all kinds left their underground homes through antholes to visit the living. For eight whole days we saw them, from a reasonable distance, because they and their attendants carried bundles of whips with which they occasionally punished themselves to prove their toughness and certainly punished you if you were available. We would keep count of the masquerades we saw every day and tally the figures at the end of the eight days and then compare our grand total with the previous year's. In a good year, the number could be well over a hundred. And the rule was that even if you saw the same masquerade ten times (as might happen with the livelier ones), you only counted it once.

And then the sounds of the village.

There was language, in song and speech, all around you. True, Christianity divided the village into two—the people of the church and the people of the world—but the boundary between them had very many crossings. The average Christian enjoyed the sights and sounds of traditional festivities. Non-Christians, for their part, observed us closely and treated some of our practices with indulgent amusement. In the most celebrated song of those days—"Egwu obi," "Song of the Heart"—they mimicked our singing in tonic sol-fa:

Ukwe ndi uka
Sss ddd m rd mr-e-e

In spoken language there was sometimes a difference in matter but none in manner between church and village. There were great orators in both. Christians of my father's generation who preached on Sundays at St. Philip's Church were not all orators, but a good number of them were. Although the Anglican Church, in a misguided effort at unification, had dealt a severe blow to the Igbo language by imposing a mechanical "union" dialect on it, the hybrid language it created remained between the covers of the Bible and was not allowed to cramp the style of sensible preachers once they had read out their obligatory text and closed the Bible. One such preacher was well known for taking to the pulpit at the time of the village feast to warn true believers against the great evil of accepting gifts of food surreptitiously over their compound wall from heathen neighbors. Obviously the traffic was heavy on the crossings. Christians had their own festivals, of course: the big one, Christmas, and the small one, Easter, although preachers kept telling you it was the other way around.

There were also two secular festivals which livened up our Christian year—Empire Day on May 24, and Anniversary on July 27.

May 24, as every schoolchild knew, was the birthday of Queen Victoria. It was a major school event and schoolchildren from all over the district would march in contingents past the British resident, who stood on a dais wearing a white ceremonial uniform with white gloves, plumed helmet, and sword.

The day's events ended with a sports competition among the schools. My first Empire Day was indeed memorable. My school, which had some very big boys and was supposed to do well in the tug-of-war, managed quite unaccountably to collapse in seconds to their opponents. Rumor had it that this was no ordinary rout but an Anglican plot whereby our headmaster had instructed our boys to give in to a fellow Anglican side to prevent a Roman Catholic victory. Empire Day celebrations took place at the provincial headquarters at Onitsha, seven miles from my village. I think it was in 1940, when I was in Standard Three and ten years old, that I was judged old enough to walk to Onitsha and back. I did it all right but could hardly get up for one week afterwards. And yet it was a journey I had looked forward to so eagerly and which I cherished for years. Onitsha was a magical place and did live up to its reputation. First of all, to look down from a high point on the road at dawn and see, four miles away, the River Niger glimmering in the sky took a child's breath away. So the river was really there! After a journey of two thousand six hundred miles from the Futa Jalon Mountains, as every schoolboy would tell you. Well, perhaps not every schoolboy. I was particularly fortunate in having parents who believed passionately in education, in having old schoolbooks that three older brothers and an older sister had read. I was good enough in my schoolwork to be nicknamed Dictionary by admirers. Although not so good in games; but no one in our culture would seriously hold that against anybody.

Two other things stand out in my mind about that first Empire Day visit to Onitsha. Cut free from my village moorings and let loose in a big city with money in my pocket, I let myself go; go so far, in fact, as to consume a half-penny worth of groundnuts. For many years afterwards the very mention of groundnuts would turn my stomach.

My other memory is much happier. I saw with my own eyes a man who was as legendary as Onitsha itself, an eccentric Englishman, Dr. J. M. Stuart Young, who had been living and trading in Onitsha since the beginning of the twentieth century. I saw him walking down New Market Road bareheaded in the sun, just as legend said he would be. The other thing legend said about Stuart Young was that he had been befriended by the mermaid of the River Niger, with whom he made a pact to remain single in return for great riches.

Later I was to learn that J. M. Stuart Young's story contained a few doubtful details, such as whether or not he did have a doctoral degree. But it was probably true that he had first come to Nigeria as a colonial civil servant and then turned against the colonial system and become a merchant intent on challenging, with African support, the monopoly of European commercial cartels. He also wrote and published poetry and fiction. Years later I was to invoke his memory and name in my short story "Uncle Ben's Choice."

The other secular event, which we called simply Anniversary, was the annual commemoration of the coming of the Gospel to Igboland, on July 27, 1857. It is reported that Bishop Adjai Crowther and his missionary team, who arrived in Onitsha on that day, were heavily beaten by rain, and as a result every Anniversary celebration since has been ruined by bad weather. Perhaps those first Anglicans did not know where the rain began to beat them! The good news is that schoolchildren were always fed new yams and stew at the Anniversary celebration. For most people it was their first taste of juicy new yam for the year.

British colonization of Nigeria was never a labor-intensive affair. White people were a rare sight, whether in the administration or the church or in commerce. This rareness did not, however, diminish their authority. The name of the British resident for Onitsha Province, Captain O'Connor, was so generally invoked that there is an age-grade named after him in Ogidi.* But I only saw him twice, from a distance. The bishop on the Niger, the Right Reverend Bishop Bertram Lasbrey, came to our church perhaps once in two or three years. His sermon left me disappointed. I don't know what I expected; perhaps I thought that if mere teachers and pastors could do as well as some that I knew, a bishop must set a congregation ablaze. But perhaps again it was the problem of having to preach through an interpreter.

---

*"Age-grade," in the Igbo tradition, is an association of people within an age bracket, functioning largely as a village group. It begins in childhood and continues throughout the duration of the individual's life. In Igbo tradition, it was unheard of for an age-grade to be named after a white man until Captain O'Connor.

Elementary education began with two years in infant school and six years in primary school. For some children there was a preschool year in what was called religious school, where they spent a year chanting and dancing the catechism.

Who is Caesar?
Siza bu eze Rom
Onye n'achi enu-uwa dum.

(Caesar is the King of Rome
Who rules the entire world.)

Who is Josiah?

Josaya nwata exe
Onye obi ya di nlo
Onatukwa egwu Chineke.

(Josiah the infant king
Whose heart was soft;
He also feared the Lord.)

But I was spared that. I suppose I imbibed adequate amounts of religion at home from the daily portions of the Bible we read at prayer time every morning and every night.

The Second World War began just as I was finishing my second year in primary school, that is, in Standard Two. The rest of my primary education happened against its distant background. But it got close one morning when two white people and their assistants came to our school and conscripted our art teacher.

I think we were loyal to Britain and did what we could to help. I remember the campaign to increase the production of palm kernels for the war effort. Our headmaster told us that every kernel we collected in the bush would buy a nail for Hitler's coffin. As the war continued, supplies for home and school became more and more scarce. Salt was severely rationed, and disappeared from the open market.

We soldiered along, singing "Rule, Britannia!," but the really popular song was "Germany Is Falling":

> Germany is falling, falling, falling
> Germany is falling to rise no more.
>
> If you are going to Germany before me
> Germany is falling to rise no more
> Tell Hitler I'm not coming there
> Germany is falling to rise no more.
>
> If you are going to Italy before me
> Tell Mussolini I'm not coming there.
>
> If you are going to Japan before me
> Tell Hirohito I'm not coming there.

The enemy list concluded, you moved on to friends whom you were naturally prepared to visit:

If you are going to England before me
Tell Churchill I am coming there.

If you are going to America before me
Tell Roosevelt I am coming there.

If you are going to Russia before me
Tell Stalin I am coming there.

If you are going to China before me
Tell Chiang Kai-shek I am coming there.

If you are going to Abyssinia before me
Tell Haile Selassie I am coming there.

Sung lustily in an arrangement for cantor and chorus, "Germany Is Falling" was as stirring as "Onward, Christian Soldiers" and other evangelical war songs.

I had two choices for secondary school—the very popular Dennis Memorial Grammar School, a C.M.S. institution in Onitsha, or Government College, Umuahia, much farther away and much less known to me. My elder brother John, a teacher who had taken me to live with him in my last year of primary school, decided I should go to Umuahia. It was not the decision I would have made myself. But John turned out to be, as usual, absolutely right.

I don't know what prompted the British colonial administration in Nigeria in the decade following the end of the First World War to set up two first-class boarding schools for boys in Nigeria, one at Ibadan and the other at Umuahia. The arguments, whatever they were, must be fascinating, but I have not been privileged to read them. Howbeit, an extraordinary English cleric, Robert Fisher, was appointed the founding principal of Government College Umuahia, and the school opened its doors in 1929. By the time Fisher retired eight years later, Umuahia was a byword in Nigeria for excellence.

Then came the Second World War, and other arguments prevailed in colonial high places, and Government College Umuahia was closed down and its buildings turned over to a prisoner-of-war camp for German and Italian nationals. There was yet a third change of colonial mind even before the war ended, and the campus was returned to education and ready to accept my generation of students in 1944. Colonial policy moved in mysterious ways!

Our new principal, William Simpson, a Cambridge man in the colonial education service, set about rebuilding the school. And what a job he did! His experience of colonial education must have persuaded him that "excessive devotion to book-work is a real danger," as he constantly intoned for our benefit, and that the cramming which often passed for education in the colonies was in fact education's greatest enemy. Though Simpson was a mathematics teacher, he made a rule which promoted the reading of novels and prohibited the reading of any textbooks after classes on three days of the week. He called it the Textbook Act. Under this draconian law, we could read fiction or biographies or magazines like *Illustrated London News* or write letters or play Ping-Pong or just sit about, but not open a textbook, on pain of detention. And we had a wonderful library from Robert Fisher's days to support Mr. Simpson's Textbook Act.

Perhaps it was a mere coincidence, but Government College Umuahia alumni played a conspicuous role in the development of modern African literature. That so many of my colleagues—Christopher Okigbo, Gabriel Okara, Elechi Amadi, Chukwuemeka Ike, I.N.C. Aniebo, Ken Saro-Wiwa, and others—should all have gone to one school would strike anyone who is at all familiar with this literature. What we read in the school library at Umuahia were the books English boys would have read in England—*Treasure Island, Tom Brown's School Days, The Prisoner of Zenda, David Copperfield,* et cetera. They were not about us or people like us, but they were exciting stories. Even stories like John Buchan's, in which heroic white men battled and worsted repulsive natives, did not trouble us unduly at first. But it all added up to a wonderful preparation for the day we would be old enough to read between the lines and ask questions. . . .

In my first or second year at Umuahia the postwar Labour government in Britain decided that a university in West Africa might not be a bad idea. So a high-powered commission under Walter Elliot was sent to survey the situation on the ground. Such was the reputation of Umuahia that the commission paid us a visit and spent a whole weekend at our school. Most of them came to chapel service on Sunday morning, but Julian Huxley, the biologist, roamed our extensive grounds watching birds with binoculars.

The Elliot Commission Report led to the foundation of Nigeria's first university institution: a university college at

Ibadan in special relationship with London. By the time it was built I was ready for university education and so walked in. By that time also I was no longer a British-Protected Child but a British Protected Person.

One of the more remarkable teachers I encountered at Ibadan was James Welch, professor of religious studies. I was intrigued by all the things he was said to have done before coming to Ibadan—head of religious broadcasting at the BBC in London; chaplain to the king; principal of a theological college. He had even gone to Nigeria before all that as a missionary in the 1930s, and then had returned to Africa at the end of the war as director of education with the British government's ill-fated East African Groundnut Scheme.

In my final year at Ibadan, I once had a chance to discuss with Professor Welch one of a growing number of disagreements the students were beginning to have with the college. He was then vice principal. In some exasperation he said to me, "We may not be able to teach you what you want or even what you need. We can only teach you what we know."

Even in exasperation, James Welch stayed calm and wise. What else can an honest and conscientious teacher teach but what he knows? The real teachers I have had in my life have been people who did not necessarily know what my needs would ultimately be but went ahead anyhow in good faith and with passion to tell me what they knew, leaving it to me to sort out whatever I could use in the search for the things that belonged to my peace. Because colonialism was essentially a denial of human worth and dignity, its education program would not be a model of perfection. And yet the great thing about being human is our ability to face adversity down by refusing to be defined by it, refusing to be no more than its agent or its victim.

What I have attempted to suggest in this rambling essay is the potency of the unpredictable in human affairs. I could have dwelt on the harsh humiliations of colonial rule or the more dramatic protests against it. But I am also fascinated by that middle ground I spoke about, where the human spirit resists an abridgement of its humanity. And this was to be found primarily in the camp of the colonized, but now and again in the ranks of the colonizer too.

The Reverend Robert Fisher was such a spirit. Technically he was of the camp of the colonizer. But such was the vision and passion he brought to his task of creating a new school at Umuahia that when he was offered a bishopric in the course of his labors he turned it down. Years later, he attempted to make light of that decision by saying he wouldn't have made a good bishop anyway. But that was not the reason. The crest he brought to Umuahia was a pair of torches, one black, one white, shining together silently. A generation later an Australian teacher added the logo *"In unum luceant"* under the emblem.

And there was William Simpson, teacher of mathematics, who would have been greatly surprised if anyone had said to him in the 1940s that he was preparing the ground for the beginnings of modern African literature.

Or even that strange Englishman J. M. Stuart Young, who opted out of the colonial system in Onitsha and set himself up in competition against his own people in giant European trading companies. His ambition to open up commerce to African traders may have seemed quixotic at the time, but the people of Onitsha admired him and gave him a big traditional funeral when he died.

These people had reached across the severe divide which colonialism would have, and touched many of us on the other side. But more important, far more important, was the fact that even if those hands had not reached across to us we would still have survived colonial tribulations, as we had done so many others before them through the millennia. That they did reach across, however, makes a great human story.

In 1976, U.S. relations with Nigeria reached an all-time low in the face of particularly clumsy American handling of the Angolan–Cuban–South African issue. Henry Kissinger, whose indifference to Africa bordered on cynicism, decided at last to meet Joseph Garba, the Nigerian foreign minister, at the United Nations. In a gambit of condescending pleasantness, Kissinger asked Garba what he thought America was doing wrong in Africa. To which Garba replied stonily: "Everything!" Kissinger's next comment was both precious and, I regret to admit, true. He said: "Statistically that is impossible. Even if it is unintentional, we must be doing something right."[2]

That exchange could easily have been about colonialism.

1993

The Sweet Aroma of Zik's Kitchen
Growing Up in the Ambience of a Legend

If you are blind, describing an elephant is easy. You can call it, like one of the six blind men in the fable, a huge tree trunk; or perhaps a gigantic fan; or an enormous rope, and so on. But having eyes, far from making such descriptions easy, actually complicates them.

So what do we do if we have to describe a phenomenon as vast as Azikiwe? Take a small part that you have a little knowledge of and tell all of it; but never pretend that what you tell is the story.

I am taking my own advice and reflecting on a very small segment of the Azikiwe story. But you can already see my difficulty in the fact that I can't seem to decide which of two titles to use; and I sense a couple more looming in the back-

In its original form, this essay was delivered as an address at Lincoln University in Pennsylvania, April 1994, at a conference honoring Dr. Nnamdi Azikiwe. The conference was hosted and sponsored by Lincoln University's president, Niara Sudarkasa.

ground—"Dr. Nnamdi Azikiwe: Zik of Africa," for example, the first president of Nigeria.

I remember, in exact and complete detail, the first day I saw Azikiwe's name in print and realized that I had been calling it wrongly all my life. I must have been about six or seven. I had gone to visit the children of one of our neighbors, a church teacher who lived three houses down the road from us. Unlike my father, who had retired from evangelical work and now lived permanently in our village on a grand pension of one pound, ten shillings a month, this neighbor was still on active missionary service and only came home to Ogidi now and again. His house, like ours, was a modern affair: mud walls and corrugated iron roof.

As I entered the front room, called the piazza in the vocabulary of missionary architecture, I saw a new almanac hanging on the wall and went immediately to look at it. I was as curious about wall hangings and posters in those days as my father was conscientious in putting new ones on our walls every year at Christmastime. A great part of my education came from those wall hangings.

But the almanac I now saw on our neighbor's wall was different from any I was familiar with at home. Ours were Church Missionary Society almanacs, with portraits of bishops and pictures of cathedrals. Our neighbor's almanac, as far as I can remember, came under the banner of ONITSHA IMPROVEMENT UNION, or something like that.

Sitting in the front row in a group photograph was Nnamdi Azikiwe in a white suit. Azikiwe was the most popular nationalist freedom fighter against colonial rule in West Africa. I read that name, "Azikiwe," over and over again in subdued surprise. I had never seen it written before, only heard it spoken. In fact, I had heard it spoken countless times, heard it invoked so often that I had come to think I knew it perfectly and was familiar with it. And now, face to face with it in print, I had suddenly realized that I never really knew it.

You see, I had up to that point called it like two names, Aziki Iwe. Two names—a foreign Christian name, Isaac, and an Igbo surname, Iwe. One of my father's friends, another retired church teacher, was called Isaac Okoye and I had assumed that "Azikiwe" was the same kind of name—until that day of enlightenment on the wall of our neighbor's house. I did not rush off to tell all my friends of my previous ignorance. I took the new knowledge in my stride, quietly, and kept news of it in my heart. It is one of the few memories I can recall in such clarity from those faraway days. And so I assume it must have been of considerable significance in my evolving consciousness.

A few years later, two or three years, maybe, I was judged old enough to take part in Empire Day celebrations in Onitsha, the famous River Niger town, seven miles away from my village. You had to be old enough in those days because if you wanted to go anywhere, you walked there. On the way to Onitsha I saw in the bush by the roadside a surveyor's concrete beacon with the legend "Professor Nnamdi Azikiwe" imprinted on it. I believe it is the same site where his house in Onitsha stands today. I may be wrong; if so, who cares? Legends are not always where you think they are.

What I want to present in a nutshell is a brief personal reminiscence of the impact of this man who bestrode the world of this child like a colossus.

It is interesting and, I believe, significant and appropriate that I became aware of him in the oral mode, pervasive and nebulous, before he crystallized into the more sedate print for me. As it happened, Azikiwe himself was as comfortable in the one mode as in the other, deploying the resources of oratory as effectively as he did the powers of print journalism.

What I am struggling to convey is elusive by its very nature—the crossroads of history and legend at a time of transition. To say that Azikiwe's name was a household word in my part of Nigeria during the first decade of my life would be true but insufficient. It was more in the general air we breathed than in the domestic chatter of our homes. There was an exhilarating touch of magic to it—a headiness, even a slight intoxication.

There is a story I heard much later, of Zik having applied when he returned from America to teach at the Yaba Higher College in Lagos and being rejected by the British colonial service. Whether this is true or not I don't know, and don't care! I like it; it ought to be true. There was an eccentric editor of the *Hansard,* the official record of parliamentary debates in Britain. One day, goes the story, an angry member of Parliament stormed into the office of this editor, threw an open copy of the paper on the table, and said to him: "I never said that!" To which the editor replied quite calmly: "I know you didn't, but you should have."

I feel the same way about Zik's application to teach at Yaba. If it didn't happen, it should have. It would offer us one great incident of poetic justice over which we can gloat and say to colonialism: *Ntoo;* served you right!

Ten years before Azikiwe, another great African nationalist had returned home to West Africa from studies in America. His name was James Kwegyir Aggrey, Dr. Aggrey of the Gold Coast. The colonial service accepted him in Achimota College, not as principal, which he deserved, but as an assistant to a nice but colorless English cleric. So Aggrey was co-opted and contained by colonial rule.

Azikiwe escaped Aggrey's fate and was able to design the strategy of his revolution—a sweeping educational project not constrained in institutions but unleashed on the streets and pathways of Nigeria's towns and villages. "Show the Light and the people will find the way." He showed and they found.

There was politics in Lagos before Zik arrived home in 1937. There were even newspapers before the *West African Pilot* brought its light. But the politics and the newspapers catered to a small coterie of well-educated, well-to-do city dwellers. It has been said that editorials in Lagos newspapers of those days were apt to be liberally spiced with long Latin quotations. Azikiwe turned his light loose among the people and transformed Nigeria overnight. Workers in government departments, teachers in missionary schools, students, clerks in European-owned commercial houses, traders in the markets—the educated and semieducated began to read newspaper stories about political freedom and the social affairs of their towns and communities. Popular singers made records eulogizing Zik nwa Jelu Oyibo, the child who journeyed to the land of the whites.

Our colonial masters were by no means novices in containing agitation among their subjects. Many school authorities banned Zik's newspapers from their institutions, which only made them doubly attractive. I went to a more enlightened school, where the teachers did not talk of banning but showed you how badly written the articles were, which was not surprising in view of the low standard of American education. I remember my English teacher in my second year setting an exam for us in which we were expected to explain such incredible words as "gubernatorial" and "eschatological." We all scored zero in that number, whereupon he revealed to us that he had taken the words straight out of a recent issue of one of Zik's papers. I suppose it was a way of telling us what a sticky end we would all come to if we followed Zik's bombastic example. It turned out, instead, to have been a very effective way of learning new English words and remembering them forever afterwards.

Those were, of course, early days in the anticolonial struggle. As Zik's influence grew, so did the measures to contain him, the most effective method ultimately being what we might call, in retrospect, the Buthelezi complex: whereby the colonizer confounds the freedom movement by sponsoring factional leaders in its ranks. This was so skillfully done in Nigeria that independence from Britain in 1960 was virtually a trap, and has remained so to this day.

This may be an appropriate time to explain the rather fanciful title of this rambling essay. I recall one of Dr. Azikiwe's First October garden parties at Government House Lagos in the early 1960s. Those were high-life days, and one of the bands that played that evening was the famous Eleazer Arinze and His Music. They played one of their best compositions, which saluted Zik the incomparable chef, the wonderful aroma of whose cooking was now floating in the wind to every corner of the land—to the north, to the east, and to the west.

The point of these lyrics, which would not have been lost on any Nigerian, was—if I may change the metaphor—that Zik had baked the cake of national independence and others had now crowded in to eat.

The lyricists may have been thinking of Zik's political rivals, but the metaphor could apply just as well to the rest of us.

When Zik returned to Nigeria in 1937, it was impossible for a Nigerian to be appointed to a senior position in the civil service. These positions were in fact called European posts.

When I graduated from University College, Ibadan, in 1953, I did not bother to look for a job; a job from broadcasting literally came to my door, looking for me. Five years later, when Azikiwe was premier of Eastern Nigeria, I was, at the ripe age of twenty-eight, controller of Eastern Region stations of the Nigerian Broadcasting Corporation. And so I understood the lyrics of sweet aroma and Zik's kitchen.

It was then I had my first brush with Nigeria's party politics. One morning as I was settling down to read the day's routine reports, my secretary announced the arrival, without any warning, of a government delegation to see me. It was indeed a high-powered delegation, comprising two cabinet ministers, the private secretary to the premier, and a somewhat vociferous leader of the youth wing of the party in power in the region. They apologized for coming without notice and promptly laid their complaint before me. My station, they said, was supporting some useless persons who had recently broken away from the government party and were now challenging it in an electioneering campaign. The reason for making this serious charge against us was that we steadily broadcast the nonsense from these people, and that I even had one of my journalists traveling with the enemy campaign team. I explained that we were following the normal methods of news gathering at our station and assured my guests that as soon as their own campaign took off we would give them even bigger coverage, because they were a bigger party. They seemed satisfied and left, but that afternoon at their national convention they passed a vote of no confidence on my station, and went further to announce their plan to end the monopoly of the Nigerian Broadcasting Corporation by setting up a regional radio and television organization to drive it out of Eastern Nigeria.

Those were rough and difficult times. We were learning painfully the rules of rudimentary democracy. The British have always claimed that they taught us the Westminster model of parliamentary democracy and we blew it. Nothing could be more absurd. You might as well say you taught someone to swim by letting him roll in the sands of the Sahara. British colonial administration was not any form of democracy, but a fairly naked dictatorship. Dr. Azikiwe, who is basically a humane democrat, was surrounded at the critical transition phase by zealots reared under colonialism with little understanding of the willing restraint demanded of those who would practice the arts of democracy.

It is quite understandable that the blind man who has spoken most about Azikiwe so far has been the student of his politics. Azikiwe's contribution to Africa's liberation politics was enormous. But to define his work simply in terms of his politics is to drastically reduce his significance. What distinguishes him from all his rivals for Nigeria's highest office and from all his successors in that position is the range and variety of his interests, enthusiasms, and accomplishments. I have already described him as a democrat and humanist. Let me mention my personal experience of him in the arts.

That same year that his party virtually declared war on the media house which I controlled was also the year in which my first novel was published. I sent a signed copy of the book to him and he sent me a most gracious letter (signed not by a secretary but by himself). And you knew he would read the book.

A few years later, when he had moved to Lagos as governor-general and I had moved also in my own little orbit, he authorized a command performance of a stage adaptation of the novel, and gave my wife and me the great privilege of sitting beside himself and his wife at the occasion.

At the risk of making this essay appear like self-advertisement rather than a celebration of Zik I must mention my receiving from his hand the first Governor-General's Trophy for my second novel at the first anniversary celebration of Nigeria's independence. That particular rite perished soon after Azikiwe inaugurated it, swept away in that flood of philistinism which seems more congenial to the mentality of Azikiwe's rivals and successors.

I must conclude on the note of Azikiwe's pan-Africanism, another feature that set him far apart from most of his fellows. From the earliest days of his journalism, he ensured the presence of the African diaspora on the pages of the *West African Pilot.* For example, anybody who read the paper got to know of George Padmore, a West Indian radical intellectual who wrote a regular and influential column there. When Azikiwe founded the University of Nigeria, Nsukka, in 1960, he named schools and colleges and departments after the distinguished African-Americans Leo Hansberry, Paul Robeson, and Washington Carver.

It is right and appropriate that Lincoln University, which started this young man on this amazing journey, should recognize in this way how far he has come.

1994

My Dad and Me

My father was born in the 1880s, when English missionaries were first arriving among his Igbo people of eastern Nigeria. He was an early convert and a good student, and by 1904 was deemed to have received enough education to be employed as a teacher and evangelist in the Anglican Mission.

The missionaries' rhetoric of change and newness resonated so deeply with my father that he called his first son Frank Okwuofu ("New Word"). The world had been tough on my father. He was an orphan child: his mother had died in her second childbirth, and his father, Achebe, a refugee from a bitter civil war in his original hometown, did not long survive his wife. My father therefore was raised not by his parents (neither of whom he remembered) but by his maternal uncle, Udoh. It was this man, as fate would have it, who received in his compound the first party of missionaries in his town. The story is told of how Udoh, a very generous and tolerant man, it seemed, finally had enough and asked his visitors to move to a public playground on account particularly of their singing, which he considered too doleful for a living man's compound. But he did not discourage his young nephew from associating with the singers, or listening to their message.

The relationship between my father and his old uncle was instructive to me. There was something deep and mystical about it, judging from the reverence I saw and felt in my father's voice and demeanor whenever he spoke about his uncle. One day in his last years he told me of a strange dream he had recently dreamt. His uncle, like a traveler from afar, had broken a long journey for a brief moment with him, to inquire how things were and to admire his nephew's "modern" house of whitewashed mud walls and corrugated iron roof.

My father was a man of few words, and I have always regretted that I had not asked him more questions. But I realize also that he took pains to tell me what he thought I needed to know. He told me, for instance, in a rather oblique way of his one tentative attempt long ago to convert his uncle. It must have been in my father's youthful, heady, proselytizing days! His uncle had said no, and pointed to the awesome row of insignia of his three titles. "What shall I do to these?" he had asked my father. It was an awesome question. What do I do to who I am? What do I do to history?

An orphan child born into adversity, heir to commotions, barbarities, rampant upheavals of a continent in disarray: was it at all surprising that he would eagerly welcome the explanation and remedy proffered by diviners and interpreters of a new word?

And his uncle Udoh, a leader in his community, a moral, open-minded man, a prosperous man who had prepared such a great feast when he took the *ozo* title that his people gave him a unique praise-name for it: was he to throw all that away now because some strangers from afar came and said so?

Those two—my father and his uncle—formulated the dialectic which I inherited. Udoh stood fast in what he knew, but he left room also for his nephew to seek other answers. The answer my father found in the Christian faith solved many problems, but by no means all.

His great gifts to me were his appreciation for education, and his recognition that whether we look at one human family or we look at human society in general, growth can come only incrementally, and every generation must recognize and embrace the task it is peculiarly designed by history and by providence to perform.

From where I stand now, I can see the enormous value of my great-uncle, Udoh Osinyi, and his example of fidelity. I also salute my father, Isaiah Achebe, for the thirty-five years he served as a Christian evangelist and for all the benefits his work and the work of others like him brought to our people. I am a prime beneficiary of the education which the missionaries had made a major component of their enterprise. My father had a lot of praise for the missionaries and their message, and so have I. But I have also learned a little more skepticism about them than my father had any need for. Does it matter, I ask myself, that centuries before these European Christians sailed down to us in ships to deliver the Gospel and save us from darkness, their ancestors, also sailing in ships, had delivered our forefathers to the horrendous transatlantic slave trade and unleashed darkness in our world?

1996

What Is Nigeria to Me?

Nigerian nationality was for me and my generation an acquired taste—like cheese. Or better still, like *ballroom* dancing. Not dancing per se, for that came naturally; but this titillating version of slow-slow-quick-quick-slow performed in close body contact with a female against a strange, elusive beat. I found, however, that once I had overcome my initial awkwardness I could do it pretty well.

Perhaps these irreverent analogies would only occur to someone like me, born into a strongly multiethnic, multilingual, multireligious, somewhat chaotic colonial situation. The first passport I ever carried described me as a "British Protected Person," an unexciting identity embodied in a phrase that no one was likely to die for. I don't mean it was entirely

In its original form, this essay was delivered as the keynote address at *The Guardian*'s Silver Jubilee, at the Nigerian Institute of International Affairs (NIIA), Victoria Island, Lagos, on October 9, 2008. It was subsequently reprinted in the *Nigeria Daily News* on October 14, 2008.

devoid of emotive meaning. After all, "British" meant you were located somewhere in the flaming red portion of the world map that covered a quarter of the entire globe in those days and was called "the British Empire, where the sun never sets." It had a good ring to it in my childhood ears—a magical fraternity, vague but vicariously glorious.

But I am jumping ahead of myself. My earliest awareness in the town of Ogidi did not include any of that British stuff, nor indeed the Nigerian stuff. That came with progress in school. Ogidi is one of a thousand or more "towns" that make up the Igbo nation, one of Nigeria's (indeed Africa's) largest ethnic groups. But the Igbo, numbering over ten million, are a curious "nation." They have been called names like "stateless" or "acephalous" by anthropologists; "argumentative" by those sent to administer them. But what the Igbo are is not the negative suggested by such descriptions but strongly, positively, in favor of small-scale political organization so that (as they would say) every man's eye would reach where things are happening. So every one of the thousand towns was a mini state with complete jurisdiction over its affairs. A sense of civic attachment to their numerous towns was more real for precolonial Igbo people than any unitary pan-Igbo feeling. This made them notoriously difficult to govern centrally, as the British discovered but never appreciated nor quite forgave. Their dislike was demonstrated during the Biafran tragedy, when they accused the Igbo of threatening to break up a nation-state they had carefully and laboriously put together.

The paradox of Biafra was that the Igbo themselves had originally championed the Nigerian nation more spiritedly than other Nigerians. One proof of this: the British had thrown more of them into jail for sedition than any others during the two decades or so of pre-independence agitation and troublemaking. So the Igbo were second to none on the nationalist front when Britain finally conceded independence to Nigeria in 1960, a move that, in retrospect, seems like a masterstroke of tactical withdrawal to achieve a supreme strategic advantage.

At the time we were proud of what we had just achieved. True, Ghana had beaten us to it by three years, but then Ghana was a tiny affair, easy to manage, compared to the huge lumbering giant called Nigeria. We did not have to be vociferous like Ghana; just our presence was enough. Indeed, the elephant was our national emblem; our airline's was the flying elephant! Nigerian troops soon distinguished themselves in a big way in the United Nations peacekeeping efforts in the Congo. Our elephant, defying aerodynamics, was flying!

Traveling as a Nigerian was exciting. People listened to us. Our money was worth more than the dollar. When the driver of a bus in the British colony of Northern Rhodesia in 1961 asked me what I was doing sitting in the front of the bus, I told him nonchalantly that I was going to Victoria Falls. In amazement he stooped lower and asked where I came from. I replied, even more casually, "Nigeria, if you must know; and, by the way, in Nigeria we sit where we like in the bus."

Back home I took up the rather important position of director of external broadcasting, an entirely new radio service aimed primarily at our African neighbors. I could do it in those days, because our politicians were yet to learn the uses of information control and did not immediately attempt to regiment our output. They were learning fast, though. But before I could get enmeshed in that, something much nastier had seized hold of all of us.

The six-year-old Nigerian federation was falling apart from the severe strain of regional animosity and ineffectual central authority. The transparent failure of the electoral process to translate the will of the electorate into recognizable results at the polls led to mass frustration and violence. While Western Nigeria, one of the four regions, was going up literally in flames, the quiet and dignified Nigerian prime minister was hosting a commonwealth conference to extricate Harold Wilson from a mess he had got himself into in faraway Rhodesia. But so tense was the local situation that the visiting heads of government had to be airlifted by helicopter from the Lagos airport into a secluded suburb to avoid rampaging crowds.

Nigeria's first military coup took place even as those dignitaries were flying out of Lagos again at the end of their conference. One of them, Archbishop Makarios of Cyprus, was in fact still in the country.

The prime minister and two regional premiers were killed by the coup-makers. In the bitter, suspicious atmosphere of the time, a naïvely idealistic coup proved a terrible disaster. It was interpreted with plausibility as a plot by the ambitious Igbo of the east to take control of Nigeria from the Hausa-Fulani north. Six months later, northern officers carried out a revenge coup in which they killed Igbo officers and men in large numbers. If it had ended there, the matter might have been seen as a very tragic interlude in nation building, a horrendous tit for tat. But the northerners turned on Igbo civilians living in the north and unleashed waves of brutal massacres, which Colin Legum of *The Observer* was the first to describe as a pogrom. It was estimated that thirty thousand civilian men, women, and children died in these massacres. Igbos were fleeing in hundreds of thousands from all parts of Nigeria to their homeland in the east.

I was one of the last to flee from Lagos. I simply could not bring myself quickly enough to accept that I could no longer live in my nation's capital, although the facts clearly said so. One Sunday morning I was telephoned from Broadcasting House and informed that armed soldiers who appeared drunk had come looking for me to test which was stronger, my pen or their gun!

The offense of my pen was that it had written a novel called *A Man of the People,* a bitter satire on political corruption in an African country that resembled Nigeria. I wanted the novel to be a denunciation of the kind of independence we were experiencing in postcolonial Nigeria and many other countries in the 1960s, and I intended it to scare my countrymen into good behavior with a frightening cautionary tale. The best monster I could come up with was a military coup d'état, which every sane Nigerian at the time knew was rather farfetched! But life and art had got so entangled that season that the publication of the novel, and Nigeria's first military coup, happened within two days of each other.

Critics abroad called me a prophet, but some of my countrymen saw it differently: my novel was proof of my complicity in the first coup.

43

I was very lucky that Sunday morning. The drunken soldiers, after leaving Broadcasting House, went to a residence I had recently vacated. Meanwhile I was able to take my wife and two little children into hiding, from where I finally sent them to my ancestral home in Eastern Nigeria. A week or two later, unknown callers asked for me on the telephone in my hideout. My host denied my presence. It was time then to leave Lagos.

My feeling towards Nigeria was one of profound disappointment. Not because mobs were hunting down and killing in the most savage manner innocent civilians in many parts of northern Nigeria, but because the federal government sat by and let it happen. The final consequence of this failure of the state to fulfill its primary obligation to its citizens was the secession of Eastern Nigeria as the Republic of Biafra. The demise of Nigeria at that point was averted only by Britain's spirited diplomatic and military support of its model colony. It was Britain and the Soviet Union which together crushed the upstart Biafran state. At the end of the thirty-month war, Biafra was a vast smoldering rubble. The cost in human lives was a staggering two million souls, making it one of the bloodiest civil wars in human history.

I found it difficult to forgive Nigeria and my countrymen and -women for the political nonchalance and cruelty that unleashed upon us these terrible events, which set us back a whole generation and robbed us of the chance, clearly within our grasp, to become a medium-rank developed nation in the twentieth century.

My immediate response was to leave Nigeria at the end

of the war, having honorably, I hoped, stayed around long enough to receive whatever retribution might be due to me for renouncing Nigeria for thirty months. Fortunately the federal government proclaimed a general amnesty, and the only punishment I received was the general financial and emotional indemnity that war losers pay, and some relatively minor personal harassment. I went abroad to New England (no irony intended), to the University of Massachusetts at Amherst, and stayed four years and then another year at the University of Connecticut. It was by far my longest exile ever from Nigeria and it gave me time to reflect and to heal somewhat. Without setting out consciously to do so, I was redefining my relationship to Nigeria. I realized that I could not reject her, but neither could it be business as usual. What was Nigeria to me?

Our 1960 national anthem, given to us as a parting gift by a British housewife in England, had called Nigeria "our sovereign motherland." The current anthem, put together by a committee of Nigerian intellectuals and actually worse than the first one, invokes the father image. But it has occurred to me that Nigeria is neither my mother nor my father. Nigeria is a child. Gifted, enormously talented, prodigiously endowed, and incredibly wayward.

Being a Nigerian is abysmally frustrating and unbelievably exciting. I have said somewhere that in my next reincarnation I want to be a Nigerian again; but I have also, in a rather angry book called *The Trouble with Nigeria,* dismissed Nigerian travel advertisements with the suggestion that only a tourist with a kinky addiction to self-flagellation would pick Nigeria for a holiday. And I mean both.

Nigeria needs help. Nigerians have their work cut out for them—to coax this unruly child along the path of useful creative development. We are the *parents* of Nigeria, not vice versa. A generation will come, if we do our work patiently and well—and given luck—a generation that will call Nigeria father or mother. But not yet.

Meanwhile our present work is not entirely without its blessing and reward. This wayward child can show now and again great intimations of affection. I have seen this flow towards me at certain critical moments.

When I was in America after the Biafran war, an army officer who sat on the council of my university in Nigeria as representative of the federal military government pressured the university to call me back home. This officer had fought in the field against my fellow Biafrans during the civil war and had been seriously wounded. He had every right to be bitter against people like me. I had never met him, but he knew my work and was himself a poet.

More recently, after a motor accident in 2001 that left me with serious injuries, I have witnessed an outflow of affection from Nigerians at every level. I am still totally dumbfounded by it. The hard words Nigeria and I have said to each other begin to look like words of anxious love, not hate. Nigeria is a country where nobody can wake up in the morning and ask: what can I do now? There is work for all.

2008

Traveling White

In October 1960, I enjoyed the first important perk of my writing career: I was awarded a Rockefeller Fellowship to travel for six months anywhere I chose in Africa. I decided to go to east, central, and southern Africa.

I set out with high hopes and very little knowledge of the real Africa. I visited Kenya, Uganda, Tanganyika, and Zanzibar, and then Northern Rhodesia and Southern Rhodesia. I had had vague notions of going to South-West Africa as well, and even South Africa itself. But Southern Rhodesia proved more than enough for me on that journey and I turned around after a little more than a week there.

The chief problem was racism. The only African country I had visited before was Ghana, the flagship of Africa's independence movement. Ghana had been independent for a few years and was justly the pride of emergent Africa. Nigeria had won her own freedom from Britain just before my journey, on

October 1, 1960, and I set forth with one month's worth of ex-colonial confidence—the wind of change, as it were, behind my sails.

The first shock came when we were about to land in Nairobi, and we were handed immigration forms to fill out. After your name, you had to define yourself more fully by filling in one of four boxes: European, Asiatic, Arab, Other! At the airport there were more of the same forms and I took one as a souvenir. I was finding the experience almost funny.

There were other minor incidents, as when the nice matronly British receptionist at the second-class hotel I checked in to in Dar es Salaam told me she didn't mind having Africans in her hotel and remembered a young West African woman who had stayed there a year or so ago and had "behaved perfectly" all the time she was there and spoke such beautiful English.

I read in the papers that a European Club in Dar was at that time debating whether it ought to amend its rules so that Julius Nyerere, who was then chief minister, might be able to accept the invitation of a member to drink there.

But as the weeks passed, my encounters became less and less amusing. I shall recount just two more, which happened in Rhodesia (modern Zambia and Zimbabwe).

I was met at Salisbury Airport by two young white academics and a black postgraduate student from the new University of Rhodesia. The Rockefeller Foundation, apparently knowing the terrain better than I did, had taken the precaution of enlisting the assistance of these literature teachers to meet me and generally keep an eye on my program. The first item on the agenda was to check in to my hotel. It turned out to be the new five-star Jameson Hotel, which had just been opened in order to avoid such international incidents as the refusal of accommodation to a distinguished countryman of mine, Sir Francis Ibiam, governor of Eastern Nigeria, president of the World Council of Churches, and a British knight!

I was neither a knight, a governor, nor president of any council, but a poor, unknown writer, traveling on the generosity of an enlightened American foundation. This generosity did not, however, stretch so far as to accommodate the kind of bills the Jameson Hotel would present.

But that was another story, which would unfold to me later. For the moment, my three escorts took me to my hotel, where I checked in and then blithely offered them a drink. It was the longest order I had or have ever made. The waiter kept going and then returning with an empty tray and more questions, the long and short of which was that the two bwanas could have their beer and so could I because I was staying in the hotel but the other black fellow could only have coffee. So I called the entire thing off. Southern Rhodesia was simply awful.

Those were not jet days, and my journey home entailed an overnight stop in Livingstone, Northern Rhodesia. The manager of the rather nice hotel where I stayed spotted me at dinner, came over and introduced himself, and sat at my table for a chat. It was a surprise; I thought he was coming to eject me. He had been manager of the Ambassador Hotel in Accra, Ghana. From him I learnt that Victoria Falls was only twenty-odd miles away and that a bus went there regularly from the hotel.

So the next morning I boarded the bus. From where I sat—next to the driver's seat—I missed what was going on in the vehicle. When finally I turned around, probably because of a certain unnatural silence, I saw with horror that everyone around me was white. As I had turned round they had averted their stony gazes, whose hostility I had felt so palpably at the back of my head. What had become of all the black people at the bus stop? Why had no one told me? I looked back again and only then took in the detail of a partition and a door.

I have often asked myself what I might have done if I had noticed the separate entrances before I boarded; and I am not sure.

Anyhow, there I was sitting next to the driver's seat in a Jim Crow bus in Her Majesty's colony of Northern Rhodesia, later to be known as Zambia. The driver (black) came aboard, looked at me with great surprise, but said nothing.

The ticket collector appeared as soon as the journey got under way. I did not have to look back anymore: my ears were now like two antennae on each side of my head. I heard a bolt move and the man stood before me. Our conversation went something like this:

TICKET COLLECTOR: What are you doing here?
CHINUA ACHEBE: I am traveling to Victoria Falls.
T.C.: Why are you sitting here?
C.A.: Why not?

T.C.: Where do you come from?

C.A.: I don't see what it has to do with it. But if you must know, I come from Nigeria, and there we sit where we like in the bus.

He fled from me as from a man with the plague. My European co-travelers remained as silent as the grave. The journey continued without further incident until we got to the falls. Then a strange thing happened. The black travelers in the back rushed out in one huge stampede to wait for me at the door and to cheer and sing my praises.

I was not elated. A monumental sadness descended on me. I could be a hero because I was in transit, and these unfortunate people, more brave by far than I, had formed a guard of honor for me!

The awesome waterfall did not revive my spirits. I walked about wrapped in my raincoat and saw the legendary sight and went back to the terminal and deliberately walked into the front of another bus. And such is the speed of hopeful news in oppressed places that nobody challenged me. And I paid my fare!

And so I never did go to South-West Africa (Namibia) in 1961. And neither did Wolfgang Zeidler twenty-five years later, for very different reasons. It is a curious little story, which came my way in 1988 when I went to lecture at the University of California at Berkeley.

A librarian there showed me a letter she had received from a friend of hers in Germany to whom she had once introduced my book *Things Fall Apart*. This friend, according to the letter, had then loaned the book to his neighbor, who was a distinguished judge. The reason for the loan was that the judge was planning with much enthusiasm to immigrate to Namibia after his retirement and accept the offer made to him to become a constitutional consultant to the Namibian regime. He planned to buy a big farm out there and spend his retirement in the open and pleasant air of the African veldt.

His neighbor, no doubt considering the judge's enthusiasm and optimism rather excessive, if not downright unhealthy, asked him to read *Things Fall Apart* on his flight to or from Namibia. Which he apparently did. The result was dramatic. In the words of the letter shown to me, the judge said that "he had never seen Africa in that way and that after having read that book he was no more innocent." And he closed the Namibia chapter.

Elsewhere in the letter, the judge was described as a leading constitutional judge in Germany; as a man with "the sharpest intelligence." For about twelve years he had been president of the Bundesverfassungsgericht, the highest constitutional court in Germany. In short, he was the kind of person the South Africans would have done much to have in their corner, a man whose presence in Namibia would give considerable comfort to the regime there. His decision not to go was obviously a triumph of common sense and humanity over stupidity and racial bigotry.

But how was it that this prominent German jurist carried such a blind spot about Africa all his life? Did he never read the papers? Why did he need an African novel to open his eyes? My own theory is that he needed to hear Africa speak for itself after a lifetime of hearing Africa spoken about by others.

I offer the story of the judge, Wolfgang Zeidler, as a companion piece to the fashionable claim made even by writers that literature can do nothing to alter our social and political condition. Of course it can!

1989

Spelling Our Proper Name

In the year 1962, even as gale-force winds of decolonization were sweeping across sub-Saharan Africa, a truly extraordinary meeting convened at Makerere University, Uganda, in East Africa.

No such conference had ever happened before; nor will its like happen again. Young African writers from newly independent nations and from countries yet to achieve freedom gathered together to discuss the goals of literature in the beautiful city of Kampala. We were all so young, so new to our task, so full of zeal and optimism.

An American visitor walked into our deliberations—venerable, even avuncular. The better informed amongst us

---

In its original form, this essay was delivered at a conference entitled "Black Writers Redefine the Struggle," on the occasion of the death of James Baldwin, at the University of Massachusetts at Amherst, April 22–23, 1988. It was subsequently published in *A Tribute to James Baldwin* (Amherst: University of Massachusetts Press, 1989) and appears here in a revised version.

said he was a famous writer, but just how famous we had no way really of knowing; our education had not run along those lines. His name was Langston Hughes. Without saying much, he seemed to preside naturally over our debate and bless our youthful zealousness with a wise benevolence. Actually, there were two visitors; the other was the tall, scholarly Saunders Redding.

A couple of years after the historic Makerere University meeting, I was awarded an open travel fellowship by UNESCO and I elected to go to the United States and Brazil. I think that the strong impression made on me by Langston Hughes—his deus ex machina appearance at that critical moment in the intellectual and literary history of modern Africa, and that unspoken message of support and solidarity after three hundred years of brutal expatriation—I think all that played a part in my choice of countries to visit. I wanted to see something of the situation of the African diaspora in its two major concentrations in the New World.

Langston Hughes showed me one more benign gesture of friendship when he heard I was in New York and invited me, a completely unknown apprentice writer, to a meal and a seat of honor beside himself at a performance of the opera *Street Scene,* for which he had written the lyrics.

There is a thread running through these introductory, anecdotal ramblings. That thread is the African/American connection. I mean "African/American" in two senses: first, as a definition of a peculiar intercontinental relationship between Africans and Americans, and second, and more importantly, as the current appellation for that person created out of mankind's greatest crime against humanity—the slave trade. There is no scale for weighing human suffering, but in sheer horror of size and scope, in its duration and the continuity of its consequence, the transatlantic slave trade was "as infinite as man may undergo." The victims of this catastrophe have been struggling for centuries now against their cruel fate on both sides of the Atlantic: on one side, scratching the soil of ruined farms in a devastated continent; on the other, toiling in the sweltering aftermath of captivity.

The nightmare lasted so long and the distances traversed were so vast that communication was breached between home and diaspora; even memory lapsed, and the two sides lost each other; they forgot who they were, their proper name. One side earned the name of slaves, and the other of savages. Oppression renames its victims, brands them as a farmer brands his cattle with a common signature. It always aims to subvert the individual spirit and the humanity of the victim; and the victim will more or less struggle to remove oppression and be free.

Unfortunately, oppression does not automatically produce only meaningful struggle. It has the ability to call into being a wide range of responses between partial acceptance and violent rebellion. In between you can have, for instance, a vague, unfocused dissatisfaction; or, worst of all, savage infighting among the oppressed, a fierce love-hate entanglement with one another like crabs inside the fisherman's bucket, which ensures that no crab gets away. This is a serious issue for African-American deliberation.

To answer oppression with appropriate resistance requires

knowledge of two kinds: in the first place, self-knowledge by the victim, which means an awareness that oppression exists, an awareness that the victim has fallen from a great height of glory or promise into the present depths; secondly, the victim must know who the enemy is. He must know his oppressor's real name, not an alias, a pseudonym, or a nom de plume!

I should like at this point to refer to two stories told by the ancestors of two different peoples in two widely separated parts of the world, perhaps more widely separated in contemporary imagination than in reality.

You remember that episode in *The Odyssey* where Odysseus tricks the Cyclops Polyphemus into calling him Noman, and how that mistake costs Polyphemus the help he might have received from his neighbors when he raises "a great and terrible cry." Of course we are not expected to shed tears for Polyphemus, for he is after all a horrible, disgusting cannibal. Nevertheless the story does make the point that in any contest—leaving aside who is right or who is wrong—an adversary who fails to recognize his opponent by his proper name puts himself at risk.

From Homer and the Greeks to the Igbo of Nigeria. There is a remarkable little story which I took the liberty of adapting to my use in *Things Fall Apart,* and which I am going to go on and adapt still further here. It is the story of Tortoise and the Birds. I will summarize it for those not familiar with my novel. The birds have been invited to a great feast in the sky, and Tortoise is pleading with them to take him along. At first they are skeptical, because they know how greedy and unreliable he is. But Tortoise manages to convince them that he is now a changed person, a born-again Tortoise, no less. So the birds agree and donate a feather each to make him a pair of wings. Not only that, they let themselves fall for Tortoise's story that it is customary on such an important outing for people to take new names. The birds have, of course, never heard of this custom but consider it rather charming and adopt it. They all take fanciful, boastful praise-names like Master of the Sky, Queen of the Earth, Streak of Lightning, Daughter of the Rainbow, and so on. The Tortoise then announces his own choice. It is very strange indeed; he is to be called You All. The birds shriek with laughter and congratulate themselves on having such a funny man on their trip.

When they arrive in the Sky and the Sky people set a great feast before them, Tortoise jumps up and asks: "Who is this feast intended for?"

"You All, of course," reply the hosts. "You heard them," says Tortoise to the birds. "The feast is for me. My name is You All."

The birds do take their revenge by repossessing their feathers and leaving Tortoise high and dry in the Sky. But that does nothing to assuage their hunger as they fly all the way back to earth on growling empty stomachs.

So the message is clear: we must not let an adversary, real or potential, assume a false name even in playfulness. It makes little difference to the victim whether the trickster calls himself Nobody, as in the Greek story, or Everybody, as in the Igbo.

Few writers have understood the ways of oppression or written more memorably about them than James Baldwin. "If you know whence you came, there is really no limit to where you can go," he tells his nephew.[1] An Igbo elder in Nigeria, using different words, might have said exactly the same thing to the youngster: "If you can't tell where the rain began to beat you, you will not know where the sun dried your body."

Literal-minded, one-track-mind people have always been exasperated by the language of prophets, as when Baldwin says to his nephew:

> You come from a long line of great poets, some of the greatest poets since Homer. One of them said: The very time I thought I was lost my dungeon shook and my chains fell off.

A bitter critic of Baldwin, Stanley Crouch, writing in *The Village Voice,* accused Baldwin of

> simplifications . . . that . . . convinced black nationalist automatons that they were the descendants of kings and queens brought in slave ships and should therefore uncritically identify with Africa.

Baldwin could never advocate an uncritical identification with anything. His mind was too good for that. He always insisted that people should weigh things for themselves and come to their own judgment:

"Take no one's word for anything, including mine," he says to his nephew, "but trust your experience."

Baldwin felt deeply, instinctively, most powerfully, the need for the African-American to know whence he came before he can know where he is headed.

The simplistic answer would be: he came from Africa, of course. Not for Baldwin, however, any simple answers. He had too much intelligence and integrity for that. "What is Africa to me?" asked an African poet who never left the motherland. Imagine, then, the tumult of questions in the soul of a man like Baldwin after three or four hundred traumatic years of absence. So in his anguished tribute to Richard Wright, he speaks of the Negro problem and the fearful conundrum of Africa.

Fearful conundrum, a terrifying problem admitting of no satisfactory solution. I am not an African-American. It would be impertinent of me to attempt to unravel that conundrum. But let me suggest two strands in its hideously tangled tissue of threads. One: the Africans sold us to Europeans for cheap trinkets. Two: Africans have made nothing of which we can be proud.

I am not sure whether or not Baldwin referred specifically to the allegation of African complicity in the slave trade. But he was seriously troubled as a young man by Africa's lack of achievement. In the famous statement in "Stranger in the Village" he contrasts his African heritage most adversely with that of a very humble European: a Swiss peasant.

The most illiterate among them is related, in a way I am not, to Dante, Shakespeare, Michelangelo, Aeschylus, Da Vinci, Rembrandt and Racine; the cathedral at Chartres says something to them which it cannot say to me, as indeed would New York's Empire State Building, should anyone here ever see it. Out of their hymns and dances came Beethoven and Bach. Go back a few centuries and they are in full glory—but I am in Africa watching the conquerors arrive.

This lament issues from a soul in torment and cannot be ignored. But before we look at it, let me say two things. First, I do not see that it is necessary for any people to prove to another that they built cathedrals or pyramids before they can be entitled to peace and safety. Flowing from that, it is not necessary for black people to invent a great fictitious past in order to justify their human existence and dignity today. What they must do is recover what belongs to them—their story—and tell it themselves.

The telling of the story of black people in our time, and for a considerable period before, has been the self-appointed responsibility of white people, and they have mostly done it to suit a white purpose, naturally. That must change and is indeed beginning to change, but not without resistance or even hostility. So much psychological, political, and economic interest is vested in the negative image. The reason is simple. If you are going to enslave or to colonize somebody, you are not going to write a glowing report about him either before or after. Rather you will uncover or invent terrible stories about him so that your act of brigandage will become easy for you to live with.

About A.D. 1600, a Dutch traveler to Benin in modern Nigeria had no difficulty comparing the city of Benin rather favorably with Amsterdam. The main street of Benin, he wrote, was seven or eight times wider than its equivalent—the Warmoes—in Amsterdam. The houses were in as good a state as the houses in Amsterdam.

Two hundred and fifty years later, before the British sacked the same city of Benin, they first described it as the "City of Blood," whose barbarism so revolted their civilized conscience that they simply had to dispatch a huge army to overwhelm it, banish its king, and loot its royal art gallery for the benefit of the British Museum and numerous private collections. All this was done, it was said with the straightest of faces, to end repugnant practices like human sacrifice. No mention whatsoever of a commercial motive—the penetration of a rich palm and rubber hinterland by British trading interests!

British penetration of West Africa in the second half of the nineteenth century was not achieved only on the field of battle, as in Benin, but at home also, in churches, schools, newspapers, novels, et cetera by the denigration of Africa and its people. The frankness of those days was nowhere better demonstrated than in an editorial by *The Times* of London expressing its outrage at the decision of Durham University to affiliate with Fourah Bay College in West Africa. *The Times* asked Durham quite pointedly if it might consider affiliating with the zoo!

Apart from the vast quantity of offensive and trashy writing about Africa in Victorian England, there also developed later a more serious "colonial genre," as biographer and historian Jeffrey Meyers calls it, beginning with Kipling in the 1880s, proceeding through Conrad to its apogee in E. M. Forster and ending with Joyce Cary and Graham Greene, even as colonialism itself began to end.

John Buchan was in the middle ground between the vulgar and the serious in this body of work. He was also interesting for combining a very senior career in the British colonial service with novel writing. What he says about natives in his novels takes on, therefore, an additional political significance. Here is what an "approved" character in his novel *Prester John* says:

> That is the difference between white and black, the gift of responsibility. . . . As long as we know and practice it we will rule not in Africa alone but wherever there are dark men who live only for their bellies.[2]

White racism in Africa, then, is a matter of politics as well as economics. The story of the black man told by the white man has generally been told to serve political and economic ends.

> Take no one's word for anything, including mine . . . know whence you came. If you know whence you came, there is really no limit to where you can go. The details of your life have been deliberately constructed to make you believe what white people say about you . . . it was intended that you should perish in the ghetto, perish by . . . never being allowed to spell your proper name.[3]

Let us now look briefly at Baldwin's "fearful conundrum" of Africans selling their brothers and sisters and children for bauble. Was that truly what happened? What about the sad, sad story of that king of the vast kingdom of Bukongo who reigned as a Christian king, Dom Afonso I, from 1506 to 1543; who built schools and churches and renamed his capital São Salvador; whose son was bishop of Utica in Tunisia and from 1521 bishop of Bukongo; who sent embassies to Lisbon and to Rome? This man thought he had allies and friends in the Portuguese Jesuits he had encouraged to come and live in his kingdom and convert his subjects. Unfortunately for him, Brazil was opening up at the same time and needing labor to work its vast plantations. So the Portuguese missionaries abandoned their preaching and became slave raiders. Dom Afonso in bewilderment wrote a letter in 1526 to King John III of Portugal complaining about the behavior of Portuguese nationals in the Congo. The letter went unanswered. In the end, the Portuguese gave enough guns to rebellious chiefs to wage war on Bukongo and destroy it, and then imposed the payment of tribute in slaves on the kingdom.

The letter Dom Afonso of Bukongo wrote to King John III of Portugal in 1526 is in the Portuguese archives and reads in part as follows:

> [Your] merchants daily seize our subjects, sons of the land and sons of our noblemen and vassals and our relatives. . . . They grab them and cause them to be sold: and so great, Sir, is their corruption and licentiousness that our country is being utterly depopulated. . . . [We] need from [your] Kingdoms no other than priests and people to teach in schools, and no other goods but wine and flour for the holy sacrament: that is why we beg of Your Highness to help and assist us in this matter, com-

manding your factors that they should send here neither merchants nor wares, because it is our will that in these kingdoms [of Congo] there should not be any trade in slaves nor market for slaves.[4]

Dom Afonso was a remarkable man. During his long reign, he learned to speak and read Portuguese. We are told that he studied the Portuguese codified laws in the original bulky folios, and criticized the excessive penalties which were inflicted for even trivial offenses. He jokingly asked the Portuguese envoy one day: "Castro, what is the penalty in Portugal for anyone who puts his feet on the ground?"[5]

Here was a man obviously more civilized than the "civilizing mission" sent to him by Europe. Radical African writers are inclined to mock him for being so willing to put aside the religion and ways of his fathers in favor of Christianity. But nobody mocks Constantine I, the Roman emperor who did precisely the same thing. The real difference is that while Constantine was powerful and succeeded, Afonso failed because the Christianity which came to him was brutal and perverse and armed with the gun. Three hundred and fifty years after Dom Afonso, Joseph Conrad was able to describe the very site on which his kingdom had stood as the Heart of Darkness.

Such stories as Dom Afonso's encounter with Europe are not found in the history books we read in schools. If we knew them, the prevailing image of Africa as a place without history until Europeans arrived would be more difficult to sustain. Young James Baldwin would not have felt a necessity to compare himself so adversely with peasants in a Swiss village. He would have known that his African ancestors did not sit through the millennia idly gazing into the horizon, waiting for European slavers to come and get them.

But ultimately Baldwin proved too intelligent to be fooled. He realized there had to be a design behind the consistent tragedy of black people. That was when he said to his nephew: "It was intended that you should perish in the ghetto."

Note the word "intended."

When I first came to the United States in the 1960s, I did not meet James Baldwin, because he had gone away to France. We finally did meet twenty years later, in Gainesville, Florida, in 1983, at a memorable event: the annual conference of the African Studies Association. During the unforgettable four days we spent down there at the conference and later visiting old slavery sites, he spoke of me in these words: "my buddy whom I met yesterday; my brother whom I met yesterday— who I have not seen in four hundred years; it was never intended that we should meet."[6]

That word again—"intended." The first order of business for Africans and their relatives, African-Americans, is to defeat the intention Baldwin speaks about. They must work together to uncover their story, whose truth has been buried so deeply in mischief and prejudice that a whole army of archaeologists will now be needed to unearth it. We must be that army on both sides of the Atlantic. The grievance against Africa some-times encountered among African-Americans must now be critically examined. The first generation of your ancestors who saw what happened firsthand should be the ones to hold a deep grudge against Africa, if there was good reason to do so.

But many of them in fact clung to Africa. Olaudah Equiano, one of the luckiest among them, acquired an education, freed himself, and wrote a book in 1789: *The Interesting Narrative of the Life of Olaudah Equiano, or Gustavus Vassa, the African. Written by Himself.* He preceded his European slave name by his original Igbo name and affirmed his African identity, waving it like a banner in the wind. When and how did the grievance begin to grow and fester? We must find out.

Equiano has been followed down the years by a band of remarkable men and women who realized in their different ways that the intention to separate us must be confounded if we are to succeed: W.E.B. DuBois, Marcus Garvey, Leo Hansberry, Chancellor Williams, Richard Wright, Langston Hughes, and a host of others. We should learn from their example.

1988

My Daughters

All my life I have had to take account of the million differences—some little, others quite big—between the Nigerian culture into which I was born, and the domineering Western style that infiltrated and then invaded it. Nowhere is the difference more stark and startling than in the ability to ask a parent: "How many children do you have?" The right answer should be a rebuke: "Children are not livestock!" Or better still, silence, and carry on as if the question was never asked.

But things are changing and changing fast with us, and we have been making concession after concession even when the other party shows little sign of reciprocating. And so I have learned to answer questions that my father would not have touched with a bargepole. And to my shame let me add that I suspect I may even be enjoying it, to a certain extent!

My wife and I have four children—two daughters and two sons, a lovely balance further enhanced by the symmetry of their arrivals: girl, boy, boy, girl. Thus the girls had taken strategic positions in the family.

We, my wife and I, cut our teeth on parenthood with the first girl, Chinelo. Naturally, we made many blunders. But Chinelo was up to it. She taught us. At age four or thereabouts, she began to reflect back to us her experience of her world. One day she put it in words: "I am not black; I am brown." We sat up and began to pay attention.

The first place our minds went was her nursery school, run by a bunch of white expatriate women. But inquiries to the school board returned only assurances. I continued sniffing around, which led me in the end to those expensive and colorful children's books imported from Europe and displayed so seductively in the better supermarkets of Lagos.

Many parents like me, who never read children's books in their own childhood, saw a chance to give to their children the blessings of modern civilization which they never had and grabbed it. But what I saw in many of the books was not civilization but condescension and even offensiveness.

Here, retold in my own words, is a mean story hiding behind the glamorous covers of a children's book:

A white boy is playing with his kite in a beautiful open space on a clear summer's day. In the background are lovely houses and gardens and tree-lined avenues. The wind is good and the little boy's kite rises higher and higher and higher. It flies so high in the end that it gets caught under the tail of an airplane that just happens to be passing overhead at that very moment. Trailing the kite, the airplane flies on past cities and oceans and deserts. Finally it is flying over forests and jungles. We see wild animals in the forests and we see little round huts in the clearing. An African village.

For some reason, the kite untangles itself at this point and begins to fall while the airplane goes on its way. The kite falls and falls and finally comes to rest on top of a coconut tree.

A little black boy climbing the tree to pick a coconut beholds this strange and terrifying object sitting on top of the tree. He utters a piercing cry and literally falls off the tree.

His parents and their neighbors rush to the scene and discuss this apparition with great fear and trembling. In the end they send for the village witch doctor, who appears in his feathers with an entourage of drummers. He offers sacrifices and prayers and then sends his boldest man up the tree to bring down the object, which he does with appropriate reverence. The witch doctor then leads the village in a procession from the coconut tree to the village shrine, where the supernatural object is deposited and where it is worshipped to this day.

That was the most dramatic of the many imported, beautifully packaged, but demeaning readings available to our children, perhaps given them as birthday presents by their parents.

So it was that when my friend the poet Christopher Okigbo, representing Cambridge University Press in Nigeria at that time, called on me and said I must write him a children's book for his company, I had no difficulty seeing the need and the urgency. So I wrote *Chike and the River* and dedicated it to Chinelo and to all my nephews and nieces.

(I am making everything sound so simple. Children may be

little, but writing a children's book is not simple. I remember that my first draft was too short for the Cambridge format, and the editor directed me to look at Cyprian Ekwensi's *Passport of Mallam Illia* for the length required. I did.)

With Chinelo, I learned that parents must not assume that all they had to do for books was to find the smartest department store and pick up the most attractive-looking book in stock. Our complacency was well and truly rebuked by the poison we now saw wrapped and taken home to our little girl. I learned that if I wanted a safe book for my child I should at least read it through and at best write it myself.

Our second daughter, Nwando, gave us a variation on Chinelo's theme eight years later. The year was 1972 and the place Amherst, Massachusetts, where I had retreated with my family after the catastrophic Biafran civil war. I had been invited to teach at the university, and my wife had decided to complete her graduate studies. We enrolled our three older children in various Amherst schools and Nwando, who was two and a half, in a nursery school. And she thoroughly hated it. At first we thought it was a passing problem for a child who had never left home before. But it was more than that. Every morning as I dropped her off she would cry with such intensity I would keep hearing her in my head all three miles back. And in the afternoon, when I went back for her, she would seem so desolate. Apparently she would have said not a single word to anybody all day.

As I had the task of driving her to this school every morning, I began to dread mornings as much as she did. But in the end we struck a bargain that solved the problem. I had to tell her a story all the way to school if she promised not to cry when I dropped her off. Very soon she added another story all the way back. The agreement, needless to say, taxed my repertory of known and fudged stories to the utmost. But it worked. Nwando was no longer crying. By the year's end she had become such a success in her school that many of her little American schoolmates had begun to call their school Nwando-haven instead of its proper name, Wonderhaven.

2009

Recognitions

The recognitions that came my way in the months of May and
June 1989 could make even a modest man like me have delu-
sions of grandeur. That spring I concluded a term of teaching
at New York's City College with a party that I was told had
been intended as a small gathering of intimate friends and colleagues at lunch but ended as a big evening affair, one of whose
amazements was the reading of a signed, sealed, and framed
proclamation issued by the president of the Borough of Man-
hattan and declaring the day of the event, May 25, Chinua
Achebe Day, "in recognition of his commitment to his art as
well as to the expression and transmission of knowledge and
truth through his writing and teaching." That was a totally
new kind of experience for me in the matter of recognitions
and immediately set my mind working on that tricky subject.

I have written previously on a countryman of mine, who
wrote a very interesting narrative of his life and published it in
London a little over two hundred years ago. His situation was

so different from mine. He had been enslaved as a child and, after many adventures, had managed to buy back his freedom and settle down in London. In presenting his book to the English public of his day, he wrote:

> It is . . . not a little hazardous in a private and obscure individ-
> ual, and a stranger too thus to solicit the indulgent attention of
> the public. . . . I am not so foolishly vain as to expect from it
> either immortality or literary reputation.

"Olaudah Equiano, or Gustavus Vassa, the African" was the flamboyant way this author identified himself on the cover of his book. The flamboyance, it must be said, was thrust upon Equiano. The editor of the 1989 reissue of his book tells us that the English naval officer who had bought him "gave him the name of Gustavus Vassa, following the condescending custom of giving slaves the names of European heroes."[1] I suppose it is rather like someone calling his cat Napoleon. Equiano fought back unsuccessfully to keep his Igbo name and finally scored partial success with that lengthy compromise. He did achieve a certain recognition, because his book went through nine editions in England between 1789 and 1797, when he died. He is today being rediscovered in Igboland and far beyond it. I have myself pinpointed to my own satisfaction and from the evidence in his text the village of his birth as Iseke. An even bolder if not outright injudicious enthusiast has gone further, to produce Equiano's present-day relations! One example of the fascination of Equiano was an international conference in Salt Lake City to commemorate the bicentennial of *The Interesting Narrative of the Life of Olaudah Equiano, or Gustavus Vassa, the African. Written by Himself.* Geography contracts; history is telescoped.

The restraint in expectations which Equiano cautions regarding immortality and literary reputation is well taken. But his extraordinary life and his record of it are clearly the stuff of great literature. Was he indeed the first writer in England to carry his books from place to place and door to door? If so, he took a major cultural practice from West Africa to Europe. If not, we may limit ourselves to calling him the stuff of legend.

Before the City College event, I had been invited by my American publishers to a booksellers' dinner in Washington, D.C. The cab ride was a capsule story of its own.

The driver turned out to be a Nigerian. He looked over his shoulder as I boarded his vehicle and called my name in the form of a question. I nodded in answer and he became so excited that he talked all the way to our destination. The other two passengers in the cab, another writer and an editor from our publishing house, just sat and watched this moving drama, which I, being partly responsible for it, tried at intervals and with little success to halt or divert. At the end of the journey, the editor held out a twenty-dollar bill to the driver. He shook his head and said that Chinua Achebe cannot pay to ride in his cab. I told him I was not paying, that my publisher was paying, and that my publisher was very rich. He still shook his head and said that Chinua Achebe's friends cannot pay in his cab!

So much for pleasant and profitable recognitions. I was to

be reminded of the other kind in a matter of days, in one of those contrasting sequences that seem to come to us by courtesy of some unseen stage director. The occasion was a visit to me by Nuruddin Farah, the Somali writer, at the International House on Riverside Drive in New York City, where I lived during my visit. He was on his way to the airport at the end of his stay at the state university branch in Stony Brook.

As we stood at the reception hall exchanging papers, one of the receptionists recognized Mr. Farah and asked excitedly if he was Nuruddin Farah, to which he replied no, he was not. You are, said the other. No, I am not, said Farah. This went on, playfully and not so playfully, for quite a while before the two finally settled the matter and rattled away in Somali.

"I never admit who I am, as a matter of principle," said Mr. Farah, a fact I was somewhat familiar with. And I knew one of the reasons, too: he had on one occasion, at least, narrowly escaped death at the hands of agents from his homeland.

So one is lucky to be able to revel in the sunshine of recognition by others. Or perhaps just naïve.

2009

Africa's Tarnished Name

It is a great irony of history and geography that Africa, whose landmass is closer than any other to the mainland of Europe, should come to occupy in the European psychological disposition the farthest point of otherness, should indeed become Europe's very antithesis. The French-African poet and statesman Léopold Sédar Senghor, in full awareness of this paradox, chose to celebrate that problematic proximity in a poem, "Prayer to Masks," with the startling imagery of one of nature's most profound instances of closeness: "joined together at the navel." And why not? After all, the shores of northern Africa and southern Europe enclose, like two cupped hands, the waters of the world's most famous sea, perceived by the ancients as the very heart and center of the world. Senghor's metaphor would have been better appreciated in the days of ancient Egypt and Greece than today.

History aside, geography has its own brand of lesson in the paradox of proximity for us. This lesson, which was probably lost on everyone else except those of us living in West Africa in the last days of the British Raj, was the ridiculous fact of longitudinal equality between London, mighty imperial metropolis, and Accra, rude rebel camp of colonial insurrection; so that, their unequal stations in life notwithstanding, they were named by the same Greenwich meridian and consequently doomed together to the same time of day!

But longitude is only half the story. There is also latitude, and latitude gives London and Accra very different experiences of midday temperature, for example, and perhaps gave their inhabitants over past eons of time radically different complexions. So differences are there, if those are what one is looking for. But there is no way in which such differences as do exist could satisfactorily explain the profound perception of alienness which Africa has come to represent for Europe.

This perception problem is not in its origin the result of ignorance, as we are sometimes inclined to think. At least, it is not ignorance entirely, or even primarily. It was in general a deliberate *invention* devised to facilitate two gigantic historical events: the Atlantic slave trade and the colonization of Africa by Europe, the second event following closely on the heels of the first, and the two together stretching across almost half a millennium from about A.D. 1500. In an important and authoritative study of this invention, two American scholars, Dorothy Hammond and Alta Jablow, show how a dramatic change in the content of British writing about Africa coincided with an increase in the volume of the slave trade to its highest level in the eighteenth century. That content shifted from almost indifferent and matter-of-fact reports of what the voyagers had seen to judgmental evaluation of the Africans. . . . The shift to such pejorative comment was due in large measure to the effects of the slave trade. A vested interest in the slave trade produced a literature of devaluation, and since the slave trade was under attack, the most derogatory writing about Africa came from its literary defenders. [Scottish slave trader Archibald] Dalzel, for instance, prefaced his work [*The History of Dahomy*] with an apologia for slavery: "Whatever evils the slave trade may be attended with . . . it is mercy . . . to poor wretches, who . . . would otherwise suffer from the butcher's knife." Numerous proslavery tracts appeared, all intent upon showing the immorality and degradation of Africans. . . . Enslavement of such a degraded people was thus not only justifiable but even desirable. The character of Africans could change only for the better through contact with their European masters. Slavery, in effect, became the means of the Africans' salvation, for it introduced them to Christianity and civilization.[1]

The vast arsenal of derogatory images of Africa amassed to defend the slave trade and, later, colonization gave the world a literary tradition that is now, happily, defunct, but also a particular way of looking (or, rather, not looking) at Africa and Africans that endures, alas, into our own day. And so, although those sensational "African" novels which were so popular in the nineteenth century and the early part of the twentieth have trickled to a virtual stop, their centuries-old obsession with lurid and degrading stereotypes of Africa has been bequeathed to the cinema, to journalism, to certain varieties of anthropology, even to humanitarianism and missionary work itself.

A few years ago, there was an extraordinary program on television about the children of the major Nazi war criminals, whose lives had been devastated by the burden of the guilt of their fathers. I remember how I felt quite sorry for them in the beginning. But then, out of nowhere, came the information that one of them had gone into the church and would go as a missionary to the Congo. I sat up.

"What has the Congo got to do with it?" I asked my television screen. Then I remembered the motley parade of adventurers, of saints and sinners that had been drawn from Europe to that region since it was first discovered by Europe in 1482— Franciscan monks, Jesuit priests, envoys from the kings of Portugal, explorers and missionaries, agents of King Leopold of the Belgians, H. M. Stanley, Roger Casement, Joseph Conrad, Albert Schweitzer, ivory hunters and rubber merchants, slave traders and humanitarians. They all made their visit and left their mark, for good or ill. And the Congo, like the ancient tree by the much used farm road, bears on its bark countless scars of the machete.

Paradoxically, a saint like Schweitzer can give one a lot more trouble than a King Leopold II, villain of unmitigated guilt, because along with doing good and saving African lives Schweitzer also managed to announce that the African was indeed his brother, but only his *junior* brother.

But of all the hundreds and thousands of European visitors to the Congo region in the last five hundred years, there were few who had the deftness and sleight of hand of Joseph Conrad, or who left as deep a signature on that roadside tree. In his Congo novella, *Heart of Darkness,* Conrad managed to transform elements from centuries of transparently crude and fanciful writing about Africans into a piece of "serious" and permanent literature.

Halfway through his story, Conrad describes a journey up the River Congo in the 1890s as though it were the very first encounter between conscious humanity, coming from Europe, and an unconscious, primeval hegemony that had apparently gone nowhere and seen nobody since the world was created. Naturally, it is the conscious party that tells the story:

> We were wanderers on a prehistoric earth, on the earth that wore the aspect of an unknown planet. We could have fancied ourselves the first of men taking possession of an accursed inheritance.[2]

"Prehistoric earth . . . unknown planet . . . fancied ourselves the first of men."

This passage, which is Conrad at his best, or his worst, according to the reader's predilection, goes on at some length through "a burst of yells," "a whirl of black limbs," "of hands clapping," "feet stamping," "bodies swaying," "eyes rolling," "black incomprehensible frenzy," "the prehistoric man himself," "the night of first ages." And then Conrad delivers his famous coup de grâce. Were these creatures really human? And he answers the question with the most sophisticated ambivalence of double negatives:

No they were not inhuman. Well, you know that was the worst of it—this suspicion of their not being inhuman.[3]

But to return to the word "fancied," which Conrad's genius had lit upon:

We could have fancied ourselves the first of men taking possession of an accursed inheritance.

I suggest that "fancied" is the alarm word insinuated into Conrad's dangerously highfalutin delirium by his genius as well as simple reason and sanity, but almost immediately crowded out, alas, by the emotional and psychological spell cast on him by the long-established and well-heeled tradition of writing about Africa. Conrad was at once a prisoner of this tradition and its most influential promoter, for he, more than anyone else, secured its admission into the hall of fame of "canonical" literature. Fancy, sometimes called Imagination, is not inimical to Fiction. On the contrary, they are bosom friends. But they also observe careful protocol around each other's property and around the homestead of their droll and difficult neighbor, Fact.

Conrad was a writer who kept much of his fiction fairly close to the facts of his life as a sailor. He had no obligation to do so, but that was what he chose to do—to write about places that actually exist and about people who live in them. He confessed in his 1917 author's note that

Heart of Darkness is experience too, but it is experience pushed a little (and only very little) beyond the actual facts of the case for the perfectly legitimate, I believe, purpose of bringing it home to the minds and bosoms of the readers.[4]

One fact of the case which Conrad may not have known was how much traffic the River Congo had already seen before it saw him in the 1890s. Even if one discounts the Africans who lived on its banks, there had been many Europeans on the river before Conrad. There was a European sailing ship on the Congo four hundred years before he made his journey, and fancied himself the first of men to do it. That degree of fancying needs a good dose of fact to go with it.

The Portuguese captain, Diogo Cão, who discovered the river for Europe in 1482 was actually looking for something else when he stumbled on it; he was looking for a passage around Africa into the Indian Ocean. On his second voyage, he went beyond his first stop up the river and heard from the inhabitants of the area about a powerful ruler whose capital was still farther up. Cão left four Franciscan monks to study the situation and resumed the primary purpose of his expedition. On his way back, he once more detoured into the Congo to pick up his monks; but they were gone! He seized, in retaliation, a number of African hostages, carried them off to Lisbon, and delivered them to King Manuel of Portugal.[5] This unpropitious beginning of Europe's adventure in the heart of Africa was quickly mended when Cão returned to the Congo for the third time in 1487, bringing back his African hostages, who had meanwhile learned the Portuguese language and Christian religion. Cão was taken to see the king, the Mweni-Congo, seated on an ivory throne surrounded by his courtiers.

Cão's monks were returned to him, and all was well. An extraordinary period ensued in which the king of Congo became a Christian with the title of Dom Afonso I. Before very long,

> the royal brothers of Portugal and Congo were writing letters to each other that were couched in terms of complete equality of status. Emissaries went back and forth between them. Relations were established between Mbanza and the Vatican. A son of the Mweni-Congo was appointed in Rome itself as bishop of his country.[6]

This bishop, Dom Henrique, had studied in Lisbon, and when he led a delegation of Congo noblemen to Rome for his consecration, he addressed the pope in Latin.

Nzinga Mbemba, baptized as Dom Afonso, was a truly extraordinary man. I have written of him elsewhere, but want to emphasize that he learned in middle life to read and speak Portuguese. It was said that when he examined the legal code of Portugal he was surprised by its excessive harshness. In jest he asked the Portuguese envoy what the penalty was in his country for a citizen who dared to put his foot on the ground! This criticism was probably reported back to the king of Portugal, for in a 1511 letter to his "royal brother," Dom Afonso, he made defensive reference to differing notions of severity between their two nations.[7] Can we today imagine a situation in which an African ruler is giving, rather than receiving, admonition on law and civilization?

The Christian kingdom of Dom Afonso I in Congo did not fare well and was finally destroyed two centuries later after a long and protracted struggle with the Portuguese. A major source of the problem was the determination of the Portuguese to take out of Congo as many slaves as their vast new colony in Brazil demanded, and the Congo kings' desire to limit or end the traffic. There was also a dispute over mining rights. In the war that finally ended the independence of the kingdom of Congo and established Portuguese control over it, the armies of both nations marched under Christian banners.

If this story reads like a fairy tale, that is not because it did not happen but because we have become all too familiar with the Africa created by Conrad's *Heart of Darkness,* its long line of predecessors going back to the sixteenth century, and its successors today, in print and the electronic media. This tradition has invented an Africa where nothing good happens or ever happened, an Africa that has not been discovered yet and is waiting for the first European visitor to explore it and explain it and straighten it up, or, more likely, perish in the attempt.

In Conrad's boyhood, explorers were the equivalent of today's Hollywood superstars. As a child of nine, Conrad had pointed at the center of Africa on a map and said: When I grow up I shall go there! Among his heroes were Mungo Park, who drowned exploring the River Niger; David Livingstone, who died looking for the source of the Nile; Dr. Barth, the first white man to approach the gates of the walled city of Kano. Conrad tells a memorable story of Barth "approaching

Kano which no European eye had seen till then," and an excited population of Africans streaming out of the gates "to behold the wonder."[8]

And Conrad also tells us how much better he liked Dr. Barth's first-white-man story than the account of Sir Hugh Clifford, British governor of Nigeria, traveling in state to open a college in Kano, forty years later. Even though Conrad and Hugh Clifford were friends, the story and pictures of this second Kano event left Conrad "without any particular elation. Education is a great thing, but Doctor Barth gets in the way."[9]

That is neatly and honestly put. The Africa of colleges is understandably of little interest to avid lovers of unexplored Africa. In one of his last essays, "Geography and Some Explorers," Conrad describes the explorers he admired as "fathers of militant geography," or even more reverentially as "the blessed of militant geography." Too late on the scene himself to join their ranks, did he become merely a militant conjurer of geography, and history? Let it be said right away that it is not a crime to prefer the Africa of explorers to the Africa of colleges. There were some good people who did. When I was a young radio producer in Lagos in the early 1960s, a legendary figure from the first decade of British colonial rule in Nigeria returned for a final visit in her eighties. Sylvia Leith-Ross had made a very important study of Igbo women in her pioneering work *African Women,* in which she established from masses of personal interviews of Igbo women that they did not fit European stereotypes of downtrodden slaves and beasts of burden.[10] She graciously agreed to do a radio program for me about Nigeria at the turn of the twentieth century. It was a wonderful program. What has stuck in my mind was when she conceded the many good, new things in the country, like Ibadan University College, and asked wistfully: "But where is my beloved bush?"

Was this the same hankering for the exotic which lay behind Conrad's preference for a lone European explorer over African education? I could hear a difference in tone. Sylvia Leith-Ross was gentle, almost self-mocking in her choice, and without the slightest hint of hostility. At worst, you might call her a starry-eyed conservationist! Conrad is different. At best, you are uncertain about the meaning of his choice. Until, that is, you encounter his portrait, in *Heart of Darkness,* of an African who has received the rudiments of education:

And between whiles I had to look after the savage who was fire-man. He was an improved specimen; he could fire up a vertical boiler. He was there below me and, upon my word, to look at him was as edifying as seeing a dog in a parody of breeches and a feather hat walking on his hind legs. A few months of training had done for that really fine chap. He squinted at the steam-gauge and at the water-gauge with an evident effort of intrepidity—and he had filed teeth too, the poor devil, and the wool of his pate shaved into queer patterns, and three orna-mental scars on each of his cheeks. He ought to have been clap-ping his hands and stamping his feet on the bank, instead of which he was hard at work, a thrall to strange witchcraft, full of improving knowledge.[11]

This is poisonous writing, in full consonance with the tenets of the slave trade–inspired tradition of European portrayal of Africa. There are endless variations in that tradition of the "problem" of education for Africa; for example, a highly educated African might be shown sloughing off his veneer of civilization along with his Oxford blazer when the tom-tom begins to beat. The moral: Africa and education do not mix. Or: Africa will revert to type. And what is this type? Something dark and ominous and different. At the center of all the problems Europe has had in its perception of Africa lies the simple question of African humanity: are they or are they not like us?

Conrad devised a simple hierarchical order of souls for the characters in *Heart of Darkness*. At the bottom are the Africans, whom he calls "rudimentary souls." Above them are the defective Europeans, obsessed with ivory, petty, vicious, morally obtuse; he calls them "tainted souls" or "small souls." At the top are regular Europeans, and their souls don't seem to have the need for an adjective. The gauge for measuring a soul turns out to be the evil character Mr. Kurtz:

> He had the power to charm or frighten rudimentary souls into an aggravated witch-dance in his honor, he could also fill the small souls of the pilgrims with bitter misgivings—he had one devoted friend at least and he had conquered one soul in the world that was neither rudimentary nor tainted with self-seeking.[12]

The alleged tendency of Africans to offer worship to any European who comes along is another favorite theme in European writing about Africa. Variations on it include the veneration by Africans of an empty Coca-Cola bottle that falls out of an airplane. Even children's stories are not free of this insult, as I once learned from foolishly buying an expensive, colorful book for my little girl without first checking it out.

The aggravated witch-dance for a mad white man by hordes of African natives may accord with the needs and desires of the fabulists of the Africa that never was, but the experience of Congo was different. Far from falling over themselves to worship their invaders, the people of this region of Africa have a long history of resistance to European control. In 1687, an exasperated Italian priest, Father Cavazzi, complained:

> These nations think themselves the foremost men in the world. They imagine that Africa is not only the greatest part of the world, but also the happiest and most agreeable. . . . [Their king] is persuaded that there is no other monarch in the world who is his equal.[13]

Between Father Cavazzi's words and Joseph Conrad's images of gyrating and babbling savages there was indeed a hiatus of two harsh centuries. But that would not explain the difference.

People are wrong when they tell you that Conrad was on the side of the Africans because his story showed great compassion towards them. Africans are not really served by his compassion, whatever it means; they ask for one thing alone—to be seen for what they are: human beings. Conrad pulls back from granting them this favor in *Heart of Darkness.* Apparently, some people can read it without seeing any problem. We simply have to be patient. But a word may be in order for those last-ditch defenders who fall back on the excuse that the racial insensitivity of Conrad was normal in his time. Even if that were so, it would still be a flaw in a serious writer—a flaw which responsible criticism today could not gloss over. But it is not even true that everybody in Conrad's day was like him. David Livingstone, an older contemporary and by no means a saint, was different. Ironically, he was also Conrad's great hero, whom he placed

> among the blessed of militant geography . . . a notable European figure and the most venerated perhaps of all the objects of my early geographical enthusiasm.[14]

And yet his hero's wise, inclusive humanity eluded Conrad. What did he think of Livingstone's famous judgment of Africans?

> I have found it difficult to come to a conclusion on their [Africans'] character. They sometimes perform actions remarkably good, and sometimes as strangely the opposite. . . . After long observation, I came to the conclusion that they are just a strange mixture of good and evil as men are everywhere else.[15]

Joseph Conrad was forty-four years *younger* than David Livingstone. If his times were responsible for his racial attitude, we should expect him to be more advanced than Livingstone, not more backward. Without doubt, the times in which we live influence our behavior, but the best or merely the better among us, like Livingstone, are never held hostage by their times.

An interesting analogy may be drawn here with the visual arts imagery of Africans in eighteenth-century Britain. I refer to a 1997 exhibition at the National Portrait Gallery in London on the subject of Ignatius Sancho, an eighteenth-century African man of letters, and his contemporaries. The centerpiece of the exhibition was the famous painting of Ignatius Sancho by Thomas Gainsborough in 1786. The art historian Reyahn King describes the painting in these words:

> Gainsborough's skill is clearest in his treatment of Sancho's skin colour. Unlike Hogarth, whose use of violet pigments when painting black faces results in a greyish skin tone, the brick-red of Sancho's waistcoat in Gainsborough's portrait, combined with the rich brown background and Sancho's own skin colour, makes the painting unusually warm in tone as well as feeling. Gainsborough has painted thinly over a reddish base with shading in a chocolate tone and minimal colder lights on Sancho's nose, chin and lips. The resulting face seems to glow and contrasts strongly with the vanishing effect so often suffered by the faces of black servants in the shadows of 18th-century portraits of their masters.[16]

Evidently Gainsborough put care and respect into his painting; and he produced a magnificent portrait of an African who had been born on a slave ship and, at the time of his sitting, was still a servant in an English aristocratic household. But neither of these facts was allowed to take away from him his human dignity in Gainsborough's portrait.

There were other portraits of Africans in Britain painted at the same time. One of them provides a study in contrasts with Gainsborough's rendering of Ignatius Sancho. The African portrayed in this other picture was one Francis Williams, a graduate of Cambridge, a poet, and a founder of a school in Jamaica: an amazing phenomenon in those days.[17] A portrait of Williams by an anonymous artist shows a man with a big, flat face lacking any distinctiveness, standing in a cluttered library on tiny broomstick legs. It was clearly an exercise in mockery. Perhaps Francis Williams aroused resentment because of his rare accomplishments. Certainly the anonymous scarecrow portrait was intended to put him in his place, in much the same way as the philosopher David Hume was said to have dismissed Williams's accomplishments by comparing the admiration people had for him to the praise they might give "a parrot who speaks a few words plainly." It is clear, then, that in eighteenth-century Britain there were Britons, like the painter Gainsborough, who were ready to accord respect to an African, even an African who was a servant; and there were other Britons, like the anonymous painter of Francis Williams, or the eminent philosopher Hume, who would sneer at a black man's achievement. And it was not so much a question of the times in which they lived as the kind of people they were. It was the same in the times of Joseph Conrad a century later, and it is the same today!

Things have not gone well in Africa for quite a while. The era of colonial freedom which began so optimistically with Ghana in 1957 would soon be captured by Cold War manipulators and skewed into a deadly season of ostensible ideological conflicts which encouraged the emergence of all kinds of evil rulers able to count on limitless supplies of military hardware from their overseas patrons, no matter how atrociously they ruled their peoples.

With the sudden end of the Cold War, these rulers or their successor regimes lost their value to their sponsors and were cast on the rubbish heap and forgotten, along with their nations. Disaster parades today with impunity through the length and breadth of much of Africa: war, genocide, military and civilian dictatorships, corruption, collapsed economies, poverty, disease, and every ill attendant upon political and social chaos! It is necessary for these sad conditions to be reported, because evil thrives best in quiet, untidy corners. In many African countries, however, the local news media cannot report these events without unleashing serious and even deadly consequences. And so the foreign correspondent is frequently the only means of getting an important story told, or of drawing the world's attention to disasters in the making or being covered up. Such an important role is risky in more ways than one. It can expose the correspondent to actual physical danger; but there is also the moral danger of indulging in sensationalism and dehumanizing the sufferer. This danger immediately raises the question of the character and attitude of the correspondent, because the same qualities of mind which in the past separated a Conrad from a Livingstone, or a Gainsborough from an anonymous painter of Francis Williams, are still present and active in the world today. Perhaps this difference can best be put in one phrase: the presence or absence of respect for the human person.

In a 1997 calendar issued by Amnesty International USA in a joint effort with the International Center of Photography, a brief but important editorial message criticizes some current journalistic practices:

> The apocalyptic vision of the newsmakers [does not] accurately document the world community. Nor are they particularly helpful in forming a picture of our common humanity.[18]

And the text goes on to set down the principles which guided the selection of the twelve photographs in the calendar, as follows:

> [They] document an authentic humanity. They also communicate the fact that every person, everywhere, possesses an inalienable rightness and an imperishable dignity—two qualities that must be respected and protected.[19]

There is a documentary film which I have seen more than once on PBS which is not troubled by Amnesty's concern. It is about sex and reproduction through the entire range of living things, from the simplest single-cell creatures in the water to complex organisms like fishes and birds and mammals. It is a very skillful, scientific production that pulls no punches with respect to where babies come from. It is all there in its starkness. Was it necessary to conclude this graphic reproductive odyssey with man (or rather woman)? I did not think so. The point had already been more than well made with apes, including, I believe, those that invented the "missionary position."

But the producers of the documentary were quite uncompromising in their exhaustiveness. And so a woman in labor *was* exposed to show the baby coming out of her. But the real shock for me was that everybody in that labor room was white except the Ghanaian (by her accent) mother in childbirth. Why were all the rest white? you may ask. Because this was all happening in a hospital in London, not in Accra.

I am sure that the producers of that program would reject with indignation any suggestion that their choice of candidate was influenced in any way by race. And they might even be right, to the extent that they would not have had a meeting of their production team to decide that a white woman would not be an appropriate subject. But then, such deliberations do not happen except perhaps in the crude caucuses of the lunatic fringe. Race is no longer a visible presence in the boardroom. But it may lie, unseen, in our subconscious. The lesson for that production team, for those who broadcast their product, and for the rest of us is that when we are comfortable and inattentive, we run the risk of committing grave injustices absentmindedly.

1998

Politics and Politicians of Language in African Literature

Of all the explosions that have rocked the African continent in recent decades, few have been more spectacular, and hardly any more beneficial, than the eruption of African literature, shedding a little light here and there on what had been an area of darkness.

So dramatic has been the change that I am even presuming that a few of my readers may recognize my title as a somewhat mischievous rendering of the subtitle of the book *Decolonising the Mind,* by an important African writer and revolutionary, Ngũgĩ wa Thiong'o. The mischief lies in my inserting after the word "politics" the two words "and politicians," like dropping a pair of cats among Ngũgĩ's pigeons.

Ngũgĩ's book argues passionately and dramatically that to speak of African literature in European languages is not only an absurdity but also part of the scheme of Western imperialism to hold Africa in perpetual bondage. He reviews his own position as a writer in English and decides that he can no longer continue in the treachery. So he makes a public renunciation of English in a short statement at the beginning of his book. Needless to say, Ngũgĩ applies the most severe censure to those African writers who remain accomplices of imperialism, especially Senghor and Achebe, but particularly Achebe, presumably because Senghor no longer threatens anybody!

Theatricalities aside, the difference between Ngũgĩ and myself on the issue of indigenous or European languages for African writers is that while Ngũgĩ *now* believes it is *either/or,* I have always thought it was *both.*

I took my stand on this from the very beginning of my literary career, and have enunciated the position at different times and in varying forms of words. No serious writer can possibly be indifferent to the fate of any language, let alone his own mother tongue. For most writers in the world, there is never any conflict—the mother tongue and the writing language are one and the same. But from time to time, and as a result of grave historical reasons, a writer may be trapped unhappily and invidiously between two imperatives. This is not new in the world. Even in the British Isles, the Irish, the Welsh, and the Scots may suffer anguish in using English, as James Joyce so memorably reminds us. Perhaps the real difference with Africa is the sheer size, the continental scale of the problem, and also—let's face it—we look quite different from the English, the French, or the Portuguese!

In 1962 we saw the gathering together of a remarkable generation of young African men and women who were to create within the next decade a corpus of writing which is today seriously read and critically evaluated in many parts of the world.

It was an enormously important moment, and year, in the history of modern African literature. The gathering took place at Makerere University, Kampala, Uganda.

The other event of 1962 was not as widely publicized as the Makerere Conference, but it was to prove at least as portentous. It was the decision by one farsighted London publisher to launch the African Writers Series on the basis of no more than three or four published titles. Conventional wisdom in the book business at the time was inclined to dismiss the whole enterprise as a little harebrained. But in the next twenty-five years this series was to publish more than three hundred titles and establish itself without any doubt as the largest and best library of African literature in existence.

It was my good fortune to be linked closely with both events. I was present in Makerere among colleagues young, hopeful, and self-assured. I heard Christopher Okigbo, who was to die four years later fighting for Biafra, declare in his high-pitched, cracked-bell voice that he wrote his poetry only for poets. Another Nigerian poet, looking around him, pronounced East Africa a cultural desert. And I heard Wole Soyinka, sitting across the hall from me, recite lines of poetic parody he had just composed in mockery of Sedar Senghor.

But it was not all plain sailing, in spite of our youth and optimism and an altogether heady confidence in our future as creative artists and in the future of our newly independent (or about-to-become-independent) nations. We had this problem of definition. What was African literature? And it was, more than anything else, a question created by the anomaly of Africans writing in European languages, a phenomenon imposed on us by a history which was peculiarly, and painfully, African. When people say to you, "Europeans write in European languages; why don't Africans write in African languages?" they are indulging in perhaps well-meaning but quite ignorant and meaningless comparison.

As for the African Writers Series in that same eventful year of 1962, I was invited to be its founding editor and I was to spend a considerable part of my literary energy in the following ten years wading through a torrent of good, bad, and indifferent writing that seemed in some miraculous way to have been waiting behind the sluice gates for the trap to be released. All of this stuff was written in English. How can one explain this?

Our acts and motives as writers seem to be in need of careful, and even repeated, explanation these days. We must justify what we do over and over again—"for the avoidance of doubt," as legal draftsmen in military regimes are fond of saying in their numerous decrees. Perhaps it is a sign of our incompetence that the case was not made clearly and unambiguously in the first instance.

The story was told me by an elder in my village about a drummer long ago who was not very competent on the drum but who managed to achieve a kind of fame by an open admission of his shortcoming. Like better drummers, he would name and salute a notable arriving at a ceremony. Having done this in drum language, our drummer would proceed, for the avoidance of doubt, to inform the person concerned by word of mouth that the drum had just saluted him.

I thought I had already spoken all the words I needed to speak on our predicament with language in African literature, but perhaps my intentions were not well enough translated to the drumsticks. So let me try again, briefly and directly.

I write in English. English is a world language. But I do *not* write in English *because* it is a world language. My romance with the world is subsidiary to my involvement with Nigeria and Africa. Nigeria is a reality which I could not ignore. One characteristic of this reality, Nigeria, is that it transacts a considerable portion of its daily business in the English language. As long as Nigeria wishes to exist as a nation, it has no choice in the foreseeable future but to hold its more than two hundred component nationalities together through an alien language, English. I lived through a civil war in which probably two million people perished over the question of Nigerian unity. To remind me, therefore, that Nigeria's foundation was laid only a hundred years ago, at the Berlin conference of European powers and in the total absence of any Africans, is not really useful information to me. It is precisely because the nation is so new and so fragile that we would soak the land in blood to maintain the frontiers mapped out by foreigners.

English is therefore not marginal to Nigerian affairs. It is quite central. I can only speak across two hundred linguistic frontiers to fellow Nigerians in English. Of course I also have a mother tongue, which luckily for me is one of the three major languages of the country. "Luckily," I say, because this language, Igbo, is not really in danger of extinction. I can gauge my good luck against the resentment of fellow Nigerians who oppose most vehemently the token respect accorded to the three major tongues by newscasters saying good night in them after reading a half-hour bulletin in English!

Nothing would be easier than to ridicule our predicament if one was so minded. And nothing would be more attractive than to proclaim from a safe distance that our job as writers is not to describe the predicament but to change it. But this is where the politics of language becomes *politicking* with language.

One year after the Makerere Conference, a Nigerian literary scholar, Obi Wali, published a magazine article in which he ridiculed the meeting and called on the African writers and the European "midwives" of their freak creations to stop pursuing a dead end. And he made the following important suggestion:

> What we would like future conferences on African literature to devote time to is the all-important problem of African writing in African languages, and all its implications for the development of a truly African sensibility.[1]

Having set that rather clear task before "future conferences on African literature," Dr. Obi Wali, who was himself a teacher of literature and a close friend of the poet Christopher Okigbo, might have been expected to lead the way along the lines of his prescription. But what he did instead was abandon his academic career for politics and business.

As a leading parliamentarian in Nigeria's Second Republic, he might have played the midwife to legislation in favor of African literature in African languages. But no: Obi Wali, having made his famous intervention, like a politician, simply dropped out of sight.

In 1966, Nigeria's first military coup triggered a countercoup and then a series of horrendous massacres of Igbo people in Hausa-speaking northern Nigeria. A famous educationist well known for his opposition to the continued use of English in Nigeria wrote in a Lagos newspaper offering the incredible suggestion that if all Nigerians had spoken one language the killings would not have happened. And he went further, to ask the Nigerian army to impose Hausa on Nigeria as its lingua franca. Fortunately, people were too busy coping with the threat of disintegration facing the country to pay serious attention to his bizarre suggestion. But I could not resist writing a brief rejoinder in which I reminded him that the thousands who had been killed did in fact speak excellent Hausa.

The point in all this is that language is a handy whipping boy to summon and belabor when we have failed in some serious way. In other words, we play politics with language, and in so doing conceal the reality and the complexity of our situation from ourselves and from those foolish enough to put their trust in us.

The politics Ngũgĩ plays with language is of a different order. It is a direct reflection of a slowly perfected Manichean vision of the world. He sees but one "great struggle between the two mutually opposed forces in Africa today: an imperialist tradition on one hand and a resistance tradition on the other." Flowing nicely from this unified vision, Africa's language problems resolve themselves into European languages, sponsored and foisted on the people by imperialism, and African languages, defended by patriotic and progressive forces of peasants and workers.

To demonstrate how this works out in practice, Ngũgĩ gives

us a moving vignette of how the enemy interfered with his mother tongue in his "Limuru peasant community":

> I was born in a large peasant family: father, four wives and about twenty-eight children. . . . We spoke Gikuyu as we worked in the fields.[2]

The reader is given nearly two pages of this pastoral idyll of linguistic and social harmony in which stories are told around the fire at the end of the day. Even at school, young Ngũgĩ is taught in Kikuyu, in which he excels to the extent of winning an infant ovation for his composition in that language. Then the imperialists struck, in 1952, and declared a state of emergency in Kenya; and Ngũgĩ's world is brutally shattered.

> All the schools run by patriotic nationalists were taken over by the colonial regime and were placed under District Education Boards chaired by Englishmen. English became the language of my formal education. In Kenya, English became more than a language: it was *the* language, and all others had to bow before it in deference.[3]

A really heartrending scenario, but also a scenario strewn with fatal snags for the single-minded. I had warned about this danger in one of the earliest statements I ever made in my literary career—that those who would canonize our past must serve also as the devil's advocate, setting down beside the glories every inconvenient fact. Unfortunately, Ngũgĩ is too good a partisan to do this double duty. So he files the totally untenable report that imperialists imposed the English language on the patriotic peasants of Kenya as recently as 1952! What about the inconvenient fact that already in the 1920s and 1930s

> the Kikuyu Independent Schools, which were started by the Kikuyu after their rift with the Scottish missionaries, *taught in English* [my italics] instead of the vernacular even in the first grade.[4]

Inconvenient though it may be, the scenario before us here is of imperialist agents (in the shape of Scottish missionaries) desiring to teach Kikuyu children in their mother tongue, while the patriotic Kikuyu peasants are revolting and breaking away because they prefer English!

What happened in Kenya also happened in the rest of the empire. Neither in India nor in Africa did the English seriously desire to teach their language to the natives. When the historic and influential Phelps-Stokes Commission report in West Africa in 1922 favored the native tongue over English, its recommendations were eagerly picked up by the official British Advisory Committee on Native Education in Tropical Africa.[5]

In Nigeria, the demand for English was already there in the coastal regions as early as the first half of the nineteenth century. A definitive study of the work of Christian missions in Nigeria from Professor J.F.A. Ajay reports that in the Niger Delta in the 1850s, the missionary teachers were already "obliged to cater for the demand . . . for the knowledge of the English language."[6]

In Calabar by 1876, some of the chiefs were not satisfied

with the amount of English their children were taught in missionary schools and were hiring private tutors at a very high fee. Nowhere in all this can we see the slightest evidence of the simple scenario painted by Ngũgĩ of European imperialism forcing its language down the throats of unwilling natives. In fact, imperialism's ways with language were extremely complex.

If imperialism was not to blame, or not entirely to blame, for the presence of European languages in Africa today, who, then, is the culprit? Ourselves? Our parents? Awkward as it may be, we should be bold enough to contemplate it and deal with it once and for all, if we can, and move on. We will discover, I am afraid, that the only reason these alien languages are still knocking about is that they serve an actual need.

No African in our recent history fought imperialism more doggedly or presided over a more progressive regime than Kwame Nkrumah of Ghana did. And yet we are told that

> during the Nkrumah era, political leaders demonstrated considerable concern over the possible divisive impact of a mother tongue policy. Although English is a language alien to Ghana they saw it as the best vehicle for achieving national communication and social and political unification.[7]

But there was a practical difficulty even more urgent than the above: the problem Ghana faced in teaching mother tongues when ethnic mixing had reached significant levels in urban and rural schools as a result of modern internal migrations. Already by 1956 the Bernard Committee had found that schools where the pupils spoke a single mother tongue were far fewer than schools in which more than five languages were represented in fair numbers. The simple consequence of this is that if the policy of teaching in mother tongues were to be enforced, the schools concerned would have to hire more than five teachers for every class. (This was at the 1956 level of ethnic mixing in Ghana. The situation today would be considerably more difficult. Unless Ghana were to reinvent bantustans and send every child back to his homeland!)

It would seem, then, that the culprit in Africa's language difficulties was not imperialism, as Ngũgĩ would have us believe, but the linguistic pluralism of modern African states. No doubt this will explain the strange fact that the Marxist states in Africa, with the exception of Ethiopia, have been the most forthright in adopting the languages of their former colonial rulers—Angola, Mozambique, Guinea-Bissau, and most lately Burkina Faso, whose minister of culture once said with a retrospective shudder that the sixty ethnic groups in that country could mean sixty different nationalities.

This does not in any way close the argument for the development of African languages by the intervention of writers and governments. But we do not have to falsify our history in the process. That would be playing politics. The words of the Czech novelist Kundera should ring in our ears: Those who seek power passionately do so not to change the present or the future but the past—to rewrite history.

There is no cause for writers to join their ranks.

1989

African Literature
as Restoration of Celebration

Many years ago, I was one of a dozen or so foreign guests at a symposium organized by the Irish Arts Council to commemorate one millennium of the City of Dublin. The general theme of that event was "literature as celebration."

Some of my colleagues, as I well recall, appeared to have difficulty with that proposition. But I, for my part, found it almost perfect for my own use; it rendered in a simple form of words a truth about art which resonated with my traditional inheritance and at the same time satisfied my personal taste in the matter. The brief paper I presented on that occasion was the germ of these reflections on African literature, a body of writing which in our lifetime has added an important dimension to world literature.

But before I start on that new literary phenomenon, I should like to repeat a disclaimer I made in Dublin. On the morning of my presentation, *The Irish Times* carried a prominent story in which a very kind columnist referred to me as the man who invented African literature. So I took the opportunity of the forum given me at the symposium to dissociate myself from that well-meant but blasphemous characterization. Now, before anyone runs away with the idea that my disavowal was due to modesty on my part, I should declare right away that I am actually not a very modest man (a fact which probably would have become transparent before very long). No, my disclaimer was an instinctive genuflection to an artistic taboo among my people, a prohibition—on pain of being finished off rather quickly by the gods—from laying proprietary hands on even the smallest item in that communal enterprise in creativity which my people, the Igbo of Nigeria, undertook from time to time, and to which they gave the name *mbari*. *Mbari* was a celebration, through art, of the world and of the life lived in it. It was performed by the community on command by its presiding deity, usually the earth goddess, Ala or Ana. Ala combined two formidable roles in the Igbo pantheon as fountain of creativity in the world and custodian of the moral order in human society. An abominable act is called *nso-ana,* "taboo to earth."

Once every so often, and in her absolute discretion, this goddess would instruct the community through divination to build a home of images in her honor. The diviner would travel through the village and knock on the doors of those chosen by Ana for her work. These chosen people were then blessed and separated from the larger community in a ritual with more than a passing resemblance to their own death and funeral. Thereafter, they moved into the forest and, behind a high fence and under the instruction and supervision of master artists and craftsmen, they constructed a temple of art.

Architecturally, it was a simple structure, a stage formed by three high walls supporting a peaked roof; but in place of a flat floor you had a deck of steps running from one side wall to the other and rising almost to the roof at the back wall. This auditorium was then filled to the brim with sculptures in molded earth and clay, and the walls painted with murals in white, black, yellow, and green. The sculptures were arranged in appropriate postures on the steps. At the center of the front row sat the earth goddess herself, a child on her left knee and a raised sword in her right hand. She is mother and judge.

To her right and left, other deities took their places. Human figures were also there, as were animals (perhaps a leopard dragging the carcass of a goat); figures from folklore, history, or pure fantasy; forest scenes, scenes of village and domestic life; everyday events, abnormal scandals; set pieces from past displays of *mbari,* new images making their debut—everything jostled together for space in that extraordinary convocation of the entire kingdom of human experience and imagination.

When all was ready, after months, or sometimes even years, of preparation, the makers of *mbari,* who had been working in complete seclusion, sent word to the larger community. A day was chosen for the unveiling and celebration of the work with music and dancing and feasting in front of the house of *mbari.*

I used the words "stage" and "auditorium" to describe the *mbari* house; let me explain. Indeed, the two side walls and the back wall encompassed a stage of sorts, comprising sculptures and paintings as actors who, after long rehearsals, are ready to perform a new celebration of art, a command performance of the earth goddess for the people assembled. But I believe the event does invite a second way of apprehension, in which the roles of stage and audience are reversed and those still and silent dignitaries of molded earth seated on the steps, and the paintings on the walls of the royal pavilion, became the spectators, and the world below a lively stage.

The problem some of my colleagues had in Dublin with the word "celebration" may have arisen, I suspect, from too narrow a perspective on it. *Mbari* extends the view, opens it out to meanings beyond the mere remembering of blessings or happy events; it deliberately sets out to include other experiences—indeed, all significant encounters which man has in his journey through life, especially new, unaccustomed, and thus potentially threatening encounters.

For example, when Europe made its appearance in Igbo society out of travelers' tales into the concrete and alarming shape of the domineering district officer, the artists of *mbari* quickly gave him a seat among the molded figures, complete with his peaked helmet and pipe. Sometimes, they even made room for his iron horse, or bicycle, and his native police orderly. To the Igbo mentality, art must, among other uses, provide a means to domesticate that which is wild; it must act like the lightning conductor which arrests destructive electrical potentials and channels them harmlessly to earth. The Igbo insist that any presence which is ignored, denigrated, denied acknowledgment and celebration, can become a focus for anxiety and disruption. To them, celebration is the acknowledgment, not the welcoming, of a presence. It is the courtesy of giving to everybody his due.

Therefore, the celebration of *mbari* was no blind adoration of a perfect world or even a good world. It was an acknowledgment of the world as these particular inhabitants perceived it in reality, in their dreams and their imagination. The white district officer was obviously not a matter for laughing or dancing. But he was not alone in that. Consider another disquieting presence: a man whose body was covered from head to toe with the spots of smallpox, a disease so dreaded that it was deified and was alluded to only in quiet, deferential tones of appeasement; it was called the Decorator of its victims, not their killer. As for the woman depicted in copulation with a dog, was there much to choose, as oddities go, between her and the white man?

I offer *mbari* as one illustration of my precolonial inheritance—of art as celebration of my reality; of art in its social dimension; of the creative potential in all of us; and of the need to exercise this latent energy again and again in artistic expression and communal, cooperative enterprises.

And now I come to what I have chosen to call my Middle Passage, my colonial inheritance. To call my colonial experience an inheritance may surprise some people. But everything is grist to the mill of the artist. True, one grain may differ from another in its powers of nourishment; still, we must, in the manner of those incomparable artists of *mbari,* accord appropriate recognition to every grain that comes our way.

It is not my intention, however, to engage in a detailed evaluation of the colonial experience, but merely to ask what possibility, what encouragement, there could be in this episode of our history for the celebration of our own world, for the singing of the song of ourselves, in the loud, insistent world and song of others.

Colonization may indeed be a very complex affair, but one thing is certain: you do not walk in, seize the land, the person, the history of another, and then sit back and compose hymns of praise in his honor. To do that would amount to calling yourself a bandit; and nobody wants to do that. So what do you do? You construct very elaborate excuses for your action. You say, for instance, that the man you dispossessed is worthless and quite unfit to manage himself or his affairs. If there are valuable things like gold or diamonds which you are carting away from his territory, you prove that he doesn't own them in the real sense of the word—that he and they just happened to be lying around the same place when you arrived. Finally, if the worse should come to the worst, you may even be prepared to question whether such as he can be, like you, fully human. It is only a few steps from denying the presence of a man standing there before you to questioning his very humanity. Therefore the agenda of the colonist did not, could not, make provision for the celebration of the world of the colonized; not even celebration of the guarded and problematic kind accorded by Africa to the white man's presence in the art of *mbari*.

I have used the word "presence" quite a few times already. Now I want to suggest that in the colonial situation "presence" was the critical question, the crucial word. Its denial was the keynote of colonialist ideology. *Question:* Were there people there? *Answer:* Well . . . not really, you know . . . people of sorts, perhaps, but not as you and I understand the word.

From the period of the slave trade, through the age of colonization to the present day, the catalogue of what Africa and Africans have been said not to have or not to be is a pretty extensive list. Churchmen at some point wondered about the soul itself. Did the black man have a soul? Popes and theologians debated that for a while. Lesser attributes such as culture and religion were debated extensively by others and generally ruled out as far as Africa was concerned. African history seemed unimaginable except, perhaps, for a few marginal places like Ethiopia, where Gibbon tells us of a short burst of activity followed from the seventh century by one thousand years in which Ethiopia fell into a deep sleep—"forgetful of the world by whom she was forgot," to use his own famous phrase.

With Hugh Trevor-Roper, Regius professor of history at Oxford in our own time, no bursts of light, no matter how brief, have ever illuminated the dark sky of the Dark Continent. A habit of generosity to Africa has not grown since Gibbon's time; on the contrary, it seems to have diminished. If we shift our focus from history to literature, we find the same hardening of attitude.

In *The Tempest,* Caliban is not specifically African; but he is the quintessential colonial subject created by Shakespeare's genius at the very onset of Europe's age of expansion. To begin with, Caliban knew not his own meaning but "wouldst gabble like a thing most brutish." However, Shakespeare restores humanity to him in many little ways, but especially by giving him not just speech but great poetry to speak before the play's end. Contrast this with Joseph Conrad's *Heart of Darkness* three hundred years later. His Calibans make "a violent babble of uncouth sounds" and go on making it right through the novel. Generosity has not prospered.

So these African creatures have no soul, no religion, no culture, no history, no human speech, no I.Q. Any wonder, then, that they should be subjugated by those who are endowed with these human gifts?

A character in John Buchan's famous colonial novel *Prester John* has this to say:

> I knew then the meaning of the white man's duty. He has to take all the risks. . . . That is the difference between white and black, the gift of responsibility, the power of being in a little way a king, and so long as we know and practice it we will rule not in Africa alone but wherever there are dark men who live only for their bellies.[1]

John Buchan, by the way, was a very senior colonial administrator and a novelist. One suspects he knew his terrain. So let us add to our long list of absences this last item—the absence of responsibility. If we should now draw a line under this list and add up all the absences reported from Africa, our grand total would equal one great absence of the Human Mind and Spirit.

I am not quite certain whether all the field workers who

reported those absences genuinely believed their report or whether it was some kind of make-believe, the kind of desperate alibi we might expect a man of conscience arraigned for a serious crime to put together. It is significant, for example, that the moment when churchmen began to doubt the existence of the black man's soul was the same moment the black man's body was fetching high prices in the marketplace for their mercantilist cousins and parishioners.

But it is also possible that these reporters actually came to believe their own stories—such was the complex psychology of the imperial vocation. The picture of Africa and Africans which they carried in their minds did not grow there adventitiously, but was planted and watered by careful social, mental, and educational husbandry. In an important study of this phenomenon, Philip Curtin tells us that Europe's image of Africa which began to emerge in the 1870s

> was found in children's books, in Sunday school tracts, in the popular press. Its major affirmations were the "common knowledge" of the educated classes. Thereafter, when new generations of explorers and administrators went to Africa, they went with a prior impression of what they would find. Most often, they found it.[2]

Conrad's famous novel *Heart of Darkness,* first published in 1899, portrays Africa as a place where the wandering European may discover that the dark impulses and unspeakable appetites he has suppressed and forgotten through ages of civilization may spring back into life in Africa's environment of free and triumphant savagery. In one striking passage, Conrad reveals a very interesting aspect of the question of presence. It is the scene where a French gunboat is sitting on the water and firing rockets into the mainland. Conrad's intention, high-minded as usual, is to show the futility of Europe's action in Africa:

> Pop would go one of the six-inch guns; a small flame would dart and vanish, a tiny projectile would give a feeble screech— and nothing happened. Nothing could happen. There was a touch of insanity in the proceeding.[3]

About sanity I cannot speak. But futility, good heavens, no! By that apparently crazy act of shelling the bush, France, at the end of the day, acquired an empire in West and equatorial Africa nine to ten times its own size. So whether there was madness in the method or method in the madness, there was profit quite definitely.

In this episode, Conrad was giving vent to one peculiar and very popular conceit: that Europe's devastation of Africa left no mark on the victim. Africa is presumed to pursue its dark, mysterious ways and destiny largely untouched by Europe's explorations and expeditions. But to deepen the mystery, Africa will sometimes assume an anthropomorphic persona, step out of the shadows, and physically annihilate the invasion—which of course adds a touch of suspense and even tragedy to Europe's enterprise. One of the best images in *Heart of Darkness* is of a boat going upstream and the forest stepping across the water to bar its return. We should note, however, that it is the African forest that takes action: the Africans themselves were absent.

It is instructive to contrast Conrad's episode of the French gunboat with the rendering of an analogous incident in *Ambiguous Adventure,* a powerful novel of colonization by the Muslim writer Cheikh Hamidou Kane, from Senegal, a West African country colonized by the French. Conrad, as we have seen, insists on the futility of the bombardment but also implies the *absence* of human response to it. Cheikh Hamidou Kane, standing as it were at the explosive end of the trajectory, tells a different story. The words are those of one of his main characters, the Most Royal Lady, a member of the Diallobe aristocracy:

> A hundred years ago our grandfather, along with all the inhabitants of this countryside, was awakened one morning by an uproar arising from the river. He took his gun and, followed by all the elite of the region, he flung himself upon the newcomers. His heart was intrepid and to him the value of liberty was greater than the value of life. Our grandfather, and the elite of the country with him, was defeated. Why? How? Only the newcomers know. We must ask them: we must go to learn from them the art of conquering without being in the right.[4]

Conrad portrays a void; Hamidou Kane celebrates a human presence and a heroic if doomed struggle.

The difference between the two stories is very clear. You

might say *that* difference was the very reason the African writer came into being. His story had been told for him, and he had found the telling quite unsatisfactory.

I went to a school modeled on British public schools. I read lots of English books there: *Treasure Island* and *Gulliver's Travels* and *Prisoner of Zenda,* and *Oliver Twist* and *Tom Brown's School Days* and such books in their dozens. But I also encountered Rider Haggard and John Buchan and the rest, and their "African" books. Africa was an enigma to me. I did not see myself as an African in those books. I took sides with the white men against the savages. In other words, I went through my first level of schooling thinking I was of the party of the white man in his hair-raising adventures and narrow escapes. The white man was good and reasonable and smart and courageous. The savages arrayed against him were sinister and stupid, never anything higher than cunning. I hated their guts.

But a time came when I reached the appropriate age and realized that these writers had pulled a fast one on me! I was not on Marlowe's boat steaming up the Congo in *Heart of Darkness;* rather, I was one of those unattractive beings jumping up and down on the riverbank, making horrid faces. Or, if I insisted on the boat ride, then I had to settle perhaps for that "improved specimen," as Conrad sarcastically calls him, more absurd, he tells us, than a dog in a pair of breeches, trying to make out the witchcraft behind the ship's water gauge. The day I figured this out was when I said no, when I realized that stories are not always innocent; that they can be used to put you in the wrong crowd, in the party of the man who has come to dispossess you.

And talking of dispossession, what about language itself? Does my writing in the language of my colonizer not amount to acquiescing in the ultimate dispossession? This is a big and complex matter which I discuss elsewhere and do not wish to go into fully here, nor evade completely. Let me simply say that when, at the age of thirteen, I went to that school modeled after British public schools, it was not only English literature that I encountered there. I came in contact also for the first time in my life with a large number of other boys of my own age who did not speak my Igbo language. And they were not foreigners but fellow Nigerian youth. We lived in the same dormitories, attended the same morning assembly and classes, and in the evenings gathered in the same playing fields. To be able to do all that, we had to put away our different mother tongues and communicate in the language of our colonizers. This paradox was not peculiar to Nigeria. It happened in every colony where the British put diverse peoples together under one administration.

Some of my colleagues, finding this too awkward, have tried to rewrite their story into a straightforward case of oppression by presenting a happy monolingual African childhood brusquely disrupted by the imposition of a domineering foreign language. This historical fantasy then demands that we throw out the English language in order to restore linguistic justice and self-respect to ourselves.

My position is that anyone who feels unable to write in English should, of course, follow his desires. But we must not take liberties with our history. It is simply not true that the English forced us to learn their language. On the contrary,

British colonial policy in Africa and elsewhere generally emphasized its preference for native languages. We saw remnants of that preference in the Bantustan policies of South Africa. The truth is that we chose English not because the British desired it but because, having tacitly accepted the new nationalities into which colonialism had forced us, we needed its language to transact our business, including the business of overthrowing colonialism itself in the fullness of time.

Now, that does not mean that our indigenous languages should be abandoned. It does mean that these languages which coexist and interact with the newcomer will increasingly do so now and into the foreseeable future. For me, it is not either English or Igbo, it is *both*. In 1967, when Christopher Okigbo, our finest poet, fell on the Biafran battlefield, I wrote for him one of the best poems I have ever written, in the Igbo language, in the form of a traditional dirge sung by young people when a member of their age group died. Some years later I wrote a different kind of poem, in English, to mark the passing of the Angolan poet and president Agostinho Neto. The ability to do both is in my view a great advantage and not the disaster some of my friends insist on calling it.

It is inevitable, I believe, to see the emergence of modern African literature as a return of celebration. It is tempting to say that this literature came to put people back into Africa. But that would be wrong, because people never left Africa, except, perhaps, in the wishful imagination of Africa's antagonists.

I must now emphasize the point I opened with. Celebration does not mean praise or approval. Of course praise and approval can be part of it, but only a part. Anyone who is familiar with contemporary African writing knows how strongly we stand in this matter; we are no flatterers of the Emperor. Some years ago at an international writers' meeting in Sweden, a Swedish writer and journalist said to a small group of us Africans present: "You fellows are lucky. Your governments put you in prison. Here in Sweden nobody pays any attention to us no matter what we write." We apologized profusely to him for his misfortune and our undeserved luck!

The running battle between the Emperor and the Poet in Africa is not a modern phenomenon, either. Our ancestral poets, the griots, had their way of dealing with the problem, sometimes direct, at other times oblique.

I shall end by telling you my adaptation of a very short Hausa tale, from Nigeria: a miniature masterpiece of the story as a two-edged sword.

The Snake was once riding his horse, curled up, as was his fashion, in the saddle. As he passed the Toad, who was walking on the road, the Toad said: "Excuse me, sir, but that is not how to ride a horse."

"It's not?" asked the Snake. "Can you show me, then, how it's done?"

"With pleasure," said the Toad.

The Snake slid out of the saddle down the side of the horse to the ground. The Toad jumped into the saddle, sat bolt upright, and galloped most elegantly up and then down the road. "That's how to ride a horse," he said.

"Very good," said the Snake. "Very good indeed. Please descend."

The Toad jumped down and the Snake slid up the side of the horse, back into the saddle, and coiled himself up as before. Then, lowering his head and looking down at the Toad on the roadside, he said: "To know is very good, but to have is better. What good can superb horsemanship do a man without a horse?" And he rode away.

Everyone can see in that simple tale the use of story to foster the status quo in a class society. The Snake is an aristocrat, who has things like horses because of who he is and not because he can ride well. The Toad is a commoner, whose horsemanship, acquired no doubt through years of struggle and practice, does not entitle him to ride in this hierarchical society. The Hausa who made this story are a monarchical people, and the ethos of the story accords well with the ruling values of their political system. One can imagine the emir and his court laughing boisterously at the telling of it.

But quite clearly, whether he was aware of it or not, the ancient griot who fashioned that piece of oral literature had concealed in the voluminous folds of its laughter the hint and the glint of iron. In the fullness of time, that same story will reveal a revolutionary purpose, using what was always there—an unattractive, incompetent, and complacent aristocracy—and exposing it not to permissive laughter but to severe stricture.

The new literature in Africa, like the old, is aware of the possibilities available to it for celebrating humanity in our continent. It is aware also that our contemporary world interlocks more and more with the worlds of others. For, as another character in *Ambiguous Adventure* says to a Frenchman:

> We have not had the same past, you and ourselves, but we shall have strictly the same future. The era of separate destinies has run its course.[5]

Whether the rendezvous of separate histories will take place in a grand, harmonious concourse or be fraught with bitterness and acrimony will all depend on whether we have learned to recognize one another's presence and are ready to accord human respect to every people.

1990

Teaching *Things Fall Apart*

I can see a number of reasons why I should be asked to contribute to the writings on how to teach *Things Fall Apart*. The first and most obvious is, of course, that I wrote the book. As obvious reasons go, this is perhaps not such a bad one. I have known the book if not more intimately then at least for a longer period than anybody else around. When people come to ask me about it, I'm reminded of journalists who ferret out the mother of a suddenly famous, or infamous, young man.

A second reason might be that I have taught literature in African and American universities for many years and should have learnt a thing or two that I could pass on. That too is a good reason. But there might even be a third and problematic one, namely, that I once gave a paper at a conference in Leeds, England, which I titled rather unwisely "The Novelist as Teacher," and as a consequence of which everything pertaining to classrooms has been referred to me ever since! And I have kept muttering: "That's not what I meant; that's not it at all!" To no effect whatsoever.

Think for a moment of that mother of a young man suddenly in the news; her attitude towards journalists ought to be—if she has sufficient *toughness*—"When I gave birth to him I fulfilled all my obligations to you. Now get out!" The Igbo wrap it more politely in a nice proverb and place it in the mouth of Mother Monkey. Says she: "I can speak for the little one inside my belly; as for the little one on my back, ask him yourself."

There is a further complication. Because I wrote *Things Fall Apart,* I have never taught it. Although I had never felt particularly disadvantaged on that score, I now realize that I cannot bring to this essay actual, concrete classroom experience, as I might do if the book in question was, shall we say, *The Palm-Wine Drinkard* or *July's People.* But my disadvantage is not, I hope, entirely crippling. For I do have other kinds of experience, garnered from years of diverse encounters with readers and critics, students and teachers. I have even, on such occasions as public lectures, attempted to reflect on some of the opinions expressed in these encounters. Letters are, of course, quite special in my view, for when a reader has been sufficiently moved (or even perturbed) by a book to sit down and compose a letter to the author, something very powerful has happened. *Things Fall Apart* has brought me a large body of such correspondence from people of different ages and backgrounds and from all the continents.

These letters have generally come singly and at leisurely

intervals. But I once received a bulky manila envelope which turned out to contain thirty-odd letters from a whole English honors class at a women's college in South Korea! They had just read *Things Fall Apart,* and been moved to write individually to me. Although I knew that the book had been making quite remarkable inroads into the Far East in recent years, I was not quite prepared for such a bumper response as the Korean letters. I hope I may be forgiven if I frame my present thoughts around some of the issues in these letters. But let me make one general point which is fundamental and essential to the appreciation of African issues by Americans. Africans are people in the same way that Americans, Europeans, Asians, et cetera, are people. Africans are not some strange beings with unpronounceable names and impenetrable minds. Although the action of *Things Fall Apart* takes place in a setting with which most Americans would be unfamiliar, the characters are normal people and their events are real human events. The necessity even to say this is part of a burden imposed on us by the customary denigration of Africa in the popular imagination of the West. I suspect that in any class of thirty American students reading *Things Fall Apart* there may be a handful who see things in the light of a certain young fellow from Yonkers, New York, who wrote to thank me several years ago for making available to him an account of the customs and superstitions of an African tribe! It should be the pleasant task of the teacher, should he or she encounter that attitude, to spend a little time revealing to the class some of the quaint customs and superstitions prevalent in America.

Fortunately not everyone in that class would be a hidebound ethnocentrist. Indeed, I should hope that there would be at least one person who resembles not the Yonkers lad or worse but another young fellow who came up to me at the University of Massachusetts, having read *Things Fall Apart* in one course or another and learning that I was on campus. He wore a very intense look and all he wanted to say was "That Okonkwo is like my father." And he was a white kid.

Now, the extraordinary thing about this is that a few years later I was to hear the very same testimony again, except that this time around it came from a very distinguished black American—James Baldwin, no less. He was responding to a question put to him at the African Literature Association Conference in Gainsville, Florida, in 1980:

> When I read *Things Fall Apart* in Paris . . . the Ibo tribe in Nigeria . . . a tribe I never saw; a system, to put it that way, or a society the rules of which were a mystery to me . . . I recognized everybody in it. That book was about my father. . . . How he got over I don't know but he did.[1]

No one can suggest that every reader or indeed that many readers of *Things Fall Apart* should come up with similar recognitions. That would make Okonkwo Everyman, which he certainly is not; he is not even Every-Igbo-Man. But it does suggest that in spite of serious cultural differences it is possible for readers in the West to identify, even deeply, with characters and situations in an African novel.

The young women from Korea responded to a very wide range of topics in the book, but I can only touch upon a few key issues which, in a way, are also representative of responses that have come to me from other quarters over the years. But there was also something I was hearing for the first time—that Koreans can draw a parallel between the colonization of the Igbo people by the British in the nineteenth century and that of their own country by Japan in the twentieth. I must say that the depth of bitterness I could glimpse from several of these letters concerning colonization was more profound than anything one encounters in Africa today. And it must have worked to unlock to these youngsters the door to Okonkwo's suffering mind and bring close a tragedy that happened so far away and long ago. And issuing out of that shared community of pain, some of them wanted to know from me why, in their own words, I let Okonkwo fail.

This question in one form or another has been repeatedly asked of me by a certain kind of reader: Why did you allow a just cause to stumble and fall? The best I can do for an answer is to say that it is in the nature of things. Which leads me directly into the carefully laid ambush of the doctrinaire: "Well, we knew you would say that. But it is not enough for us that our art should merely report the nature of things; it should aim to change it."

I agree of course about good art changing things. But it doesn't go about it with the uncomplicated, linear equivalency of *sympathetic magic* that would send its practitioner scouring the forest for spotted leaves to cure a patient who has broken out in spots. That is not medicine but charlatanism.

Good causes can and do fail even when the people who

espouse and lead them are not themselves in one way or another severely flawed.

This is of course the stuff of tragedy in literature, with its many intricate ways of affecting us which I cannot get into here. But I do want to suggest that the concepts of success and failure as commonly used in this connection are inadequate. Did Okonkwo fail? In a certain sense, obviously yes. But he also left behind a story strong enough to make those who hear it even in faraway Korea wish devoutly that things had gone differently for him. More than one Korean student took issue with me over the manner of his dying. Again this is a matter that has come up before in discussions and in criticism. I don't know what Korean traditional culture teaches about suicide. Western culture, we know, views it as a species of moral cowardice, or simply as a "copping out," thus trivializing it into a matter between an individual and his problems. In Okonkwo's world it is a monumental issue between an individual on the one hand and, on the other, society and all its divinities, including titulary gods and ancestors—indeed, the entire cosmos. A suicide puts himself beyond every conceivable pale. Okonkwo is a rash man, and it is unlikely that he has reasoned out the Igbo saying that the thought which leads a man to kill himself cannot be merely one night old. Events have been urging him towards total rupture with his world.

Finally, when this world crumbles so miserably and so disgracefully under attack, Okonkwo, who has never learnt to live with failure, separates himself from it with ultimate eschatological defiance.

While on the subject of last things, I might as well bring up in conclusion the question of the very last words of the novel, which, as I recall, used to embroil critics in considerable argument. The distinguished American scholar and teacher Jules Chametzky opens his book *Our Decentralized Literature* with a discussion of that aspect of the novel. Since his point agrees completely with what I might call the narrative intention of the story's ending, I shall save my breath and quote somewhat lengthily from it:

> In the last paragraph of Chinua Achebe's *Things Fall Apart*—perhaps the most memorable account in English of an African culture and the impact on it of white European encroachment—the voice and language of the book shifts with startling abruptness. . . . Anyone who has read or taught this novel can testify to the outrageous reductionism of this last paragraph, especially its last sentence. It is chilling, but ultimately fulfills the enlightening effort of the whole book. Obviously it forces us to confront the "Rashomon" aspect of experience—that things look different to different observers and that one's very perceptions are shaped by the social and cultural context out of which one operates.[2]

That about sums up the mission of *Things Fall Apart,* if a novel could be said to have a mission.

1991

Martin Luther King and Africa

I did not have the good fortune of meeting Martin Luther King, but his work, his thought, and his death left a strong feeling that this man belonged to Africa in a very special sense—a sense that goes far beyond the fact that his ancestors were brought to America from Africa, important as that fact may be. Martin Luther King had no choice in his involvement in the Atlantic slave trade, but he did make a choice—and an emphatic one—to embrace the pain and suffering of the African continent. His vision of an America in which the structures of racism must be challenged and brought down by sheer moral force began early in Dr. King's life to incorporate the problems of Africa and its people.

In preparation for his work, Dr. King had cultivated many

This essay originated as a talk given at the King Holiday Celebration, January 20, 1992, at the Smithsonian Institution National Museum of Natural History in Washington, D.C.

friendships and personal relationships with African students in America. In 1957, he and his wife journeyed to Africa to be present at the independence celebrations of Kwame Nkrumah's Ghana, that flagship of modern Africa's voyage into political freedom. Dr. King was only twenty-eight years old at that time. I shall return shortly to the often forgotten fact of Dr. King's youth and precocity. For the moment I want to stress his eagerness to forge close ties with African leaders in all parts of the continent: Albert Luthuli in South Africa, Ahmed Ben Bella in the north, Kwame Nkrumah in the west, Tom Mboya in the east, Kenneth Kaunda in south-central, and so on. Dr. King had gone for progressive leaders in strategic locations.

In 1957, the same year that he attended Ghana's independence, Dr. King, with Eleanor Roosevelt and Bishop James Pike, sponsored a document signed by 130 world leaders urging the international community to protest against apartheid. In 1962, he sponsored with Albert Luthuli an "Appeal for Action Against Apartheid," an early call for sanctions against South Africa, whose political system he described as "a medieval segregation organized with twentieth-century efficiency and drive; a sophisticated form of slavery."

Why was it that Martin Luther King, in preparation for his great work in these United States, made so much commitment so early to the fortunes of Africa? Why did he not evince that debilitating ambivalence which so many African-Americans show towards Africa or suffer that awkwardness which so many of us Africans and African-Americans suffer in each other's presence, that historical alienation which James Baldwin in his early days had called "the African conundrum," with the suggestion of a bitter, immemorial grievance.

I bring in James Baldwin to these reflections because he was so uncompromisingly brilliant and clear-eyed, with such an uncommon gift of eloquence in defining our condition and for spelling our proper name. But even he had had this "problem" with Africa and had been so exasperated by it that in his earlier days he once lamented the "fact" that his African ancestors did nothing but sit around waiting for white slavers to arrive!

If that picture of African history was anywhere close to what happened, quite clearly Africa would have to accept the responsibility for an unnatural and indescribable crime for which "conundrum" would be a generous understatement. For we are talking about the transatlantic slave trade, that horrendous event which Basil Davidson, the distinguished British historian, has called "the greatest and most fateful migration— forced migration—in the history of man," and which others might go further and call the greatest crime against humanity in the history of the world.

Some time ago, in a heated TV discussion on multiculturalism and curriculum content, a professor of history from a prestigious American university in an abrupt switch of focus declared that it was Africans who captured their own people in the hinterland and sold them to white people on the coast. He didn't say what the whites were doing on the African coast thousands of miles from their own homes. Perhaps we are to believe that the whites were holidaying on Africa's sunny beaches! We must put fairy tales aside and resume our search for the truth. Not only from excellent schools and schoolmen, for they can be so disappointing. Basil Davidson frankly admits the problem. "The records are copious," he writes, "but mainly they are European records and they are colored indelibly by the myth and prejudice which the [slave] trade itself did so much to promote."[1]

It is that problem that has bequeathed to the world the conventional wisdom in which we have all been "educated": a scenario in which the victim is blamed for the crime—either for his inferiority, which once was held to justify it, or his participation, which is now touted as the cause of it.

Fortunately, truth is rarely completely lost or irrecoverable. Even in the very archives of Europe, there are entries here and there that point us in more hopeful and rational directions. In the archives of Portugal, for example, there are moving appeals from the king of Congo to his "royal brother" the king of Portugal to restrain Portuguese slavers in the African kingdom.

Through the long night of the slave-trading centuries, skeptical voices questioning the conventional wisdom of their times also lightened the darkness in sporadic flashes. For example, when Thomas Jefferson compared Negroes to whites and concluded that Negroes were inferior in all but memory, that Euclid was beyond their reasoning powers, and that in imagination they were "dull, tasteless and anomalous," another American, one Imlay White, told him respectfully that nothing could be

more uncertain and false than estimating and comparing the intellect and talents of two descriptions of men: one enslaved, degraded and fettered . . . the other free, independent and with the advantage of appropriating the reason and science which have been the result of the study and labors of the philosophers and sensible men for centuries back.[2]

That unequal exchange, favoring Jefferson in fame and public esteem and Imlay White in quality of argument, demonstrates in my view the hope and attractiveness of American life, its stubborn promise, not always fulfilled but ready to reenter the fray between reason and canon.

Two decades after Baldwin's terrible comment on his African ancestors, he and I finally met in 1980 for the first, and sadly last, time at the annual conference of the African Literature Association in Gainesville, Florida. He had obviously come to see the conventional attitudes to his ancestors and their history for what they were. In a public dialogue between us he called me "a brother I have not seen in 400 years" and added emotionally: "It was never intended that we should meet."[3] In other words, there was a third party implicated in our soured relationship.

Martin Luther King either did not suffer Baldwin's kind of anguish about his African connection or else got over it very early and very fast. And it was just as well, because as we all know now he was not to be allowed too much time. I said at the beginning that we often forget how young King was when he died. *Thirty-nine!* And we are not talking about a champion athlete or boxer who must achieve his peak early, but a thinker/activist who must grow, meditate on his mission, and mature into action. Mahatma Gandhi at the age of thirty-nine had not even returned to India!

King learned from Gandhi that human beings have a fundamental obligation to respect life even in the thick of a just struggle, for if they should forget or suspend this obligation and violate the lives of others, they would cheapen their own lives and their very humanity. But these thoughts could just as well have come to Martin Luther King out of the great Bantu dictum on humanity's indivisibility: *Umuntu ngumuntu nqabantu,* "A human is human because of other humans." We cannot trample upon the humanity of others without devaluing our own. The Igbo, always practical, put it concretely in their proverb *Onye ji onye n'ani ji onwe ya:* "He who will hold another down in the mud must stay in the mud to keep him down." How much of African thoughts and memories—half forgotten, disguised, or repressed—lives on in the minds and hearts of African-Americans, we shall never know.

If you ask me what I think makes Martin Luther King worthy of the honor and celebration we accord his memory today, I will say it is two things: what he achieved himself, and what he stands for in a long line of a people's struggle for freedom and justice.

First, his personal achievement. I am not concerned here about marches and boycotts, great and important though they were, but rather about a man who struggled to conquer in himself both fear and hate, two of humanity's most destructive and limiting emotions. I want to stress *struggled* and *conquered.* The struggling is as important as the conquering, perhaps more, because it is *that*—the fact that the outcome was never a foregone conclusion, that our hero did not enter the stage fully formed and destined to win; that he began where most of us stand today, vulnerable to fear and prejudice and all the other frailties of our human condition; and yet he struggled and won victories—it is that which makes us kin to the hero and enables us to become beneficiaries of his heroic journey and able to derive from it the energy and hope to dare the obstacles on our own little side roads. That is what Martin Luther King should say to each of us, individually.

Second, he is important as a staging post in a long history of black struggle going back to the first revolts, and as a signpost for future battles. It is important to have this historical perspective, because it is the correct one and because it saves us from the heresy that there was once a golden age of tyranny when its victims were quite happy with their oppression.

A white American missionary, J. Lowrie Anderson, working in Nairobi, reported an incident which took place between him, another American, and a Kenyan soon after King's assassination:

> As a colleague and I sat down to tea with an African friend he said bitterly: "We hate you Americans. You killed our Martin Luther King." My colleague replied: "Yes, I was ashamed of being an American—until I remembered that Martin Luther King was an American also. Then I was proud."

It is appropriate that we celebrate Martin Luther King, a man who struggled so valiantly to restore humanity to the oppressed and the oppressor.

1992

The University and the
Leadership Factor in Nigerian Politics

There is a story about Bernard Shaw arriving at the New York harbor in the days of sea travel, stepping off the ship, and being immediately mobbed by journalists. But before even the quickest of them could open his mouth, Bernard Shaw had fired off his response and stopped them cold: Don't ask me what you should do to be saved; the last time I was here I told you and you haven't done it!

I feel very much like that about this whole national debate business which our military has imposed on us. We know what we should do and we refuse to do it. Instead, we are going about "blowing grammar" all over the place, as if our problem stemmed from insufficient shouting. So I turned down or simply ignored all invitations to join the charade. But then the University of Nigeria asked me to participate in a debate "organized solely for a university as an integral community in the Nigerian family, expected to be in the mainstream and not in the periphery of Nigerian affairs." I couldn't quite say no to this particular call, having coming as it does from my very backyard.

And I was asked specifically to reflect on the problem of leadership, on which my stand is probably well known in Nigeria; so the forum's organizers seemed to be inviting me to answer some well canvassed criticisms of that stand. It was altogether too enticing!

My little book *The Trouble with Nigeria,* published on the eve of President Shehn Shagari's second term, opens with the following words:

> The trouble with Nigeria is simply and squarely a failure of leadership. There is nothing basically wrong with the Nigerian character. There is nothing wrong with the Nigerian land or climate or water or air or anything else. The Nigerian problem is the unwillingness or inability of its leaders to rise to the responsibility, to the challenge of personal example which is the hallmark of true leadership.

So the question of leadership was and is preeminent, in my mind, among Nigeria's numerous problems. The little book does go on to identify others, such as tribalism, corruption, indiscipline, social injustice, indulgence for mediocrity, et cetera. But my thesis is that without good leadership none of the other problems stands a chance of being tackled, let alone solved.

Now, the twin criticisms of my stand which I find sufficiently interesting to want to answer are: (1) that my view of the Nigerian predicament is elitist, because it emphasizes the role of a crop of leaders rather than of the broad masses; and (2) that my diagnosis wrongly identifies people rather than economic and political systems as the source of the Nigerian problem.

I do recognize, of course, that there are broadly three components to the equation for national development: system, leader, and followers. In an ideal world, each would mesh nicely and efficiently with the others. But quite clearly Nigeria is not in such a world, not even on the road to it. She seems in fact to be going in the opposite direction, towards a world of bad systems, bad leadership, and bad followership. The question then is, How do we redirect our steps in a hurry? In other words, where do we begin and have the best chance of success? To change the Nigerian system; to change the Nigerian leadership style; or to change the hearts of one hundred and twenty million Nigerians?

Proponents of the supremacy of system would argue that unless you have the right political-economic arrangement no good leader can emerge or survive and certainly no good followership can develop. I am no stranger to the allure of this argument, and I admit it can be engaging, especially when it is presented by first-class minds. I remember hearing C.L.R. James (author of *The Black Jacobins*) at a memorable lecture he gave at the University of Massachusetts making a case for systems. James was a bold and erudite Marxist thinker and was putting forward the rather startling argument that during the Great Depression America had a choice of following one of two eminent citizens—Franklin D. Roosevelt or Paul Robeson. Roosevelt, he said, had proposed to tinker with the traumatized American capitalist system, while Paul Robeson, a more brilliant person by far, stood for scrapping the system altogether. Of course America followed Roosevelt and cast Robeson on the rubbish heap. And the result, said C.L.R. James, was Watergate, a scandal that was deeply exercising America at the time of his lecture. And then with typical hyperbole James told his spellbound audience that even if Jesus Christ and his disciples were to descend and take over the running of the American White House there still would have been Watergate!

What he was saying, in effect, was not only that the American capitalist system was unviable but that systems were all that mattered. And that was plainly doctrinaire. Roosevelt's New Deal programs of social reconstruction and his restructuring of American financial institutions, especially the creation of the Federal Deposit Insurance Corporation (FDIC), may not today be called the revolutions some people thought they were at the time, but anybody who would dismiss them as mere tinkering would have to be a very committed adversary indeed! And he would have to demonstrate, not merely through intellectual abstractions but by pointing to an actual system in practice somewhere which can show better results and no scandals of one form or another.

In my view the basic problem with efforts to bestow preeminence on systems is, however, their inability to explain how an abstract system can bring itself into being autonomously. Would it drop from the sky and operate itself? Would Tanzania have chosen the socialist path to development if Nyerere had not been around? And, next door, would Kenya have gone capitalist if Oginga Odinga rather than Kenyatta had been leader? When fellows speak glibly about the right system, they forget that they are talking about political arrangements brought into being either evolutionally or revolutionally in other places and times by leaders of those times and places or their forerunners. It would not have occurred to Lenin or Castro (to use just two examples) to dismiss the leadership factor in thinking systems out and converting abstract social models into actual institutions. These are inescapable roles of intellectual and political leadership.

Of course, one could argue that all the thinking that needs to be done in this matter has already been done elsewhere by other people and that we, the latecomers, do not need to reinvent the wheel, as it were. But that is a proposition we could not live with.

We need not spend too long on the argument for the preeminence of followers. It is enough to say that no known human enterprise has flourished on the basis of followers leading their leaders. The cliché that people get the leader they deserve is a useful exaggeration—useful because it reminds the general populace of the need for vigilance in selecting their leaders (where they have a chance to do so) and for keeping them under constant surveillance.

But to go beyond that and suggest, as one has often heard people do in this country, that when a leader misleads or fails to offer any leadership at all it is because Nigerians are unpatriotic and impossible to govern, or that when a leader accepts a bribe he is no more to blame than the man who offered the bribe, is completely to misunderstand the meaning of leadership.

Leadership is a sacred trust, like the priesthood in civilized, humane religions. No one gets into it lightly or unadvisedly, because it demands qualities of mind and discipline of body and will far beyond the need of the ordinary citizen. Anybody who offers himself or herself or is offered to society for leadership must be aware of the unusually high demands of the role and should, if in any doubt whatsoever, firmly refuse the prompting.

Sometimes one hears apologists of poor leadership ask critics whether they would do better if they were in the shoes of the leader. It is a particularly silly question, the answer to which is that the critic is not in or running for the leader's shoes, and therefore how he might walk in them does not arise. An editorial writer can surely condemn a pilot who crashes an airplane through carelessness or incompetence, or a doctor who kills his patient by negligent administration of drugs, without having to show that he can pilot a plane or write prescriptions himself.

The elite factor is an indispensable element of leadership. And leadership itself is indispensable to any association of human beings desirous of achieving whatever goals it sets for itself.

When such an association is engaged in a difficult undertaking or is in pursuit of a risky objective such as nation building, the need for competent leadership becomes particularly urgent. It is like having the captain who takes control over those "who go down to the sea in ships" or up into the clouds in airplanes. Even a nation already firmly established will in times of emergency allow unprecedented powers to its leader, no matter how deeply its democratic instincts may run in normal times. During the Great Depression, the fiercely independent-minded industrial/business complex in America virtually handed its affairs over to President Roosevelt.

When we speak of leadership, we generally are thinking of political leadership. This is to be expected, because under normal circumstances political institutions provide the overarching structure of human society. But there are other kinds of leadership operating under the political superstructure: military/industrial, intellectual, artistic, religious, et cetera. Each of these subgroups evolves its own peculiar rules and chain of command, from the top through a more or less restricted core of middle managers down to the mass of followers. This model can of course be described as elitist.

Unfortunately "elitist" has become a dirty word in contemporary usage. It was inevitable and indeed desirable that with the spread of democratic principles in the world, elite systems inherited from mankind's immemorial past should be subjected, like any other received values and practices, to critical scrutiny and reappraisal. But in a world in which easy sloganeering so quickly puts the critical faculty to flight, what has happened to the word "elite" is a good example of how a once useful word can become manipulated to a point where it no longer facilitates thought but even inhibits it. But perhaps the cloud under which the word has come is not entirely undeserved. A word is more likely to become abused when the concept it represents has been corrupted.

I should like to examine briefly the uses and abuses of the elite system, using the example of a national army. An army is, of course, one of those branches of human organization where the need for clear, unambiguous leadership exists. The line of command is both necessary and rigid. Even the armies of "people's democracies" have not succeeded in obliterating the line between the commander and the commanded.

Now, in addition to the inescapable fact of hierarchy in their organization, most modern armies have devised special, elite corps of troops whose job is to move in and smash particularly difficult obstacles and move out again, leaving the regular forces to carry on routine military activities. Members of such an elite corps are rated much higher than regular troops and are given all kinds of special favors and perquisites to compensate them for the extraordinary exertions they make and dangers they face.

But supposing an army were to recruit its elite corps not on the highest and toughest standards of soldiering but because they were the children of generals and admirals, it would have created a corrupt elite corps pampered with special favors without having the ability of storm troopers. So the real point about an elite is not whether it is necessary or not but whether it is genuine or counterfeit. This boils down to how it is recruited. And this will be true of any elite system. An elite corps of scientists is indispensable to the modern state, but if its recruitment is from the children and brothers-in-law of professors rather than from young scientists of the greatest talent, it would be worse than useless, because it would not only fail to produce scientific results itself but would actually inhibit such results from other quarters. A counterfeit elite, in other words, inflicts double jeopardy on society.

So the real problem posed by leadership is that of recruitment. Political philosophers from Socrates and Plato to the present time have wrestled with it. Every human society, including our own traditional and contemporary societies, has also battled with it. How do we secure the services of a good leader?

A magazine columnist who doesn't share my view on this matter published a picture of me with my chin resting on my hand and a caption below saying: "Achebe waiting for the Messiah." Most unfair, of course! But even so, waiting for a messiah may not be as far-fetched or ludicrous as the columnist may imagine. For we have no fail-safe prescription for bringing the great leader into being. No people have had a monopoly in this. Great leaders have arisen in diverse places from every conceivable system: feudal, democratic, revolutionary, military, et cetera. Kemal Atatürk, Chaka, Elizabeth I, Lenin, Mao, Lincoln, Nkrumah.

Does it mean, then, that like the iroko tree the great leader will grow where he will and that the rest of us should just sit, put our hand under our chin, and wait? No! If we cannot compel greatness in our leaders, we can at least demand basic competence. We can insist on good, educated leaders while we wait and pray for great ones. Even divine leaders have needed precursors to make straight their way.

In traditional monarchical systems such as we would today dismiss as anachronistic, there were elite groups called king-makers whose business was to keep an eye on all the eligible princes and choose the best when the time came. These king-makers were specially qualified by tradition and by knowledge of the history of the kingdom, and no less by being themselves ineligible for selection so that they could be seen to be reason-ably disinterested. Those of us who often doubt that we could learn anything from our traditional systems and usage should compare the scrupulousness of the kingmaker arrangement with the lack of it in our elections today!

Be that as it may, the universities and other elite centers with deep knowledge of national and world issues can play a role somewhat analogous to that undertaken by kingmakers of the past, not in selecting the king themselves but by spreading in advance general enlightenment and a desire for excellence in the entire constituency of the nation, including those who will aspire to national leadership.

We must admit that the Nigerian university has not acquit-ted itself too brilliantly in this regard in the past. The univer-sity man who has sallied forth into national politics has had a rather dismal record. No one can point to any shining achieve-ment in national politics which the nation can recognize as the peculiar contribution of university men and women. Rather, quite a few of them have been splashed with accusations of abuse of office and other forms of corruption.

Those who have not sallied forth but remained in the ivory tower have hardly fared better. Many have cheapened them-selves and eroded their prestige by trotting up and down between the campus and the waiting rooms of the powerful, vying for attention and running one another down for the entertainment of the politician. For this and other reasons, the university has deservedly lost its mystique and squandered the credibility which it had in such abundance at the time of Nigeria's independence.

To cap it all, we have had a zealous policy maker from the highest level of university administration whose sole preoccupation was a balancing act of applying the wealth of the nation to keep back the go-ahead, and reward and pamper the sluggard, in a mistaken and futile effort to achieve unity through discrimination, and parity in backwardness.

Who, then, is to champion that pursuit of excellence on which the university ideal is founded and which no people can neglect without paying a heavy price in stagnation and decay? The Nigerian university has so far shown little faith in its own mission. Is it any wonder that others should be lukewarm?

One remarkable feature of Nigeria used to be that no one who ruled it in its first quarter century had been to university. Did that say anything about our national preoccupations and values? Look around us and compare our record in this regard with that of our neighbors, even in Africa.

I do not suggest that the university is the only fountain of enlightenment and excellence. Far be it from me to suggest that. But not to have had one university man in eight, and not once in twenty-six years! Our traditional people would have sought the offices of *Afa* divination to explain that!

As the twenty-first century takes hold of us, we must take a hard look at ourselves and ask why the intellectual leadership which the Nigerian nation deserves to get from the university has not been forthcoming. It is imperative that the Nigerian university set about cleaning up its act. It must go back to work so as to produce that salt of excellence which the nation relies on it to drop into the boiling soup pot of Nigerian leadership.

1988

Stanley Diamond

I was intrigued to be asked to contribute a paper to a volume of essays in honor of Stanley Diamond. Dialectical anthropology is not a field in which I can wander freely and at ease. My accustomed turf is elsewhere. But I assume there was a reason for asking me; and for that very reason (if I have divined it correctly) I couldn't refuse or let the occasion pass without a single word.

Stanley Diamond came to Biafra. In fact, he came twice during the terrible civil war that ravaged Nigeria from 1967 to 1970. For many of us embattled there, his coming meant so much. Why? He was only one of so many visitors we had. What made his coming so special?

Biafra had stirred deep emotions across the world. It probably gave television evening news its first chance to come into its own and invade without mercy the sacrosanctity of people's living rooms with horrifying scenes of children ground to dust by modern war—a surrogate war fought with modern weapons. Said Baroness Asquith in the British House of Lords: "Thanks to the miracle of television we see history happening before our eyes. We see no Ibo propaganda; we see the facts."[1]

If governments were largely unmoved by the tragedy, ordinary people were outraged. I witnessed from the visitors' gallery of the House of Commons what was described as unprecedented rowdiness during a private member's motion on Biafra. Harold Wilson, villain of the piece, sat as cool as a cucumber, leaving his foreign secretary, Michael Stewart, to sweat it out.

It was hardly surprising that many remarkable people would want to visit the scene of such human tragedy. Auberon Waugh came, and afterwards wrote a devastating book on Britain's duplicitous policy. He also named his newborn child Biafra Waugh! Frederick Forsyth, a mere reporter then, was soon sacked by his employer, the BBC, for filing stories too favorable to Biafra. Count Carl Gustaf von Rosen, the Swedish nobleman who became a legend in the 1930s when he volunteered to fight for Haile Selassie against the Italians, came back to Africa to embrace Biafra's cause and threw Nigeria's air force of MiG and Ilyushin fighters into disarray and panic with five tiny two-seater Minicon planes.

There was an American Air Force colonel (retired)—I cannot now recall his name—who came out of his retirement in Florida to fly food and medical supplies on behalf of Joint Church Aid from the Portuguese island of São Tomé into Biafra. He flew many missions into Uli airport—a segment of highway the Biafrans had converted with great ingenuity into a landing strip, camouflaged during the day with leaves and transformed into one of Africa's busiest airports at night. One stormy night, the colonel did not make it back. I called on his widow during a visit I made to Florida. It was a painful meeting. I didn't really know the man and there was nothing I could say to this woman who sat so calm and courteous but remote. But before I took my leave she asked her question: "Tell me honestly, did he do any good coming?"

"Yes," I said. "Definitely. He saved a few children." She smiled then with tears in her eyes.

There was a small group of American writers who came to show solidarity with Biafra's beleaguered writers—Kurt Vonnegut, Herbert Gold, and Harvey Swados. They barely got out again before Biafra's final collapse and the closure of the airport. Each of these visitors and scores of others, many of whom I did not meet or know about, came in answer to the call of a common humanity. They came to the losers. I was told that when von Rosen heard of the defeat of Biafra he said it would take the world fifty years at least to understand what had happened.

Stanley Diamond came like all these others. But he also brought something additional—a long-standing scholarly interest and expertise in the territory. In her book *The World and Nigeria: The Diplomatic History of the Biafran War, 1967–1970*, Suzanne Cronje, onetime diplomatic correspondent of the *Financial Times* of London, makes the following point: "On the whole, the emphasis on suffering and the relief of it damaged Biafra's chances of gaining international recognition. The problem came to be regarded as a humanitarian rather than a political dilemma; it was easier to donate money for milk than to answer Biafra's international challenge."[2]

Stanley Diamond knew Nigeria well, having done extensive fieldwork in parts of it right from the last days of the British Raj, and followed its affairs closely through independence and after. He understood the ideological dimension of the conflict. He was not fooled by the strenuous effort of Britain to pass off her former colony as a success story of African independence when in fact it had only passed, with Britain's active collaboration, from colonial to neocolonial status. He saw the bloody civil war not as Britain and other apologists for Nigeria presented it—that is, progressive nationalism fighting primitive tribalism—but as the ruining of a rare and genuine national culture at the moment of its birth.

It was advantageous to the federal Nigerian case to stigmatize Biafra for its alleged links with South Africa and Portugal. Stanley Diamond pointed out that in the first year of the war it was the Czechoslovakians and the Chinese, not South Africa or Portugal, who supplied the bulk of Biafra's arms purchases, and that the Czech source dried up after the crushing of the Prague Spring reform movement by Soviet tanks and the fall of Alexander Dubček in 1968.

When the moment comes for us to ask the proper questions and draw the right inferences about what happened in those terrible years, the perceptions of Stanley Diamond will be a great help to us. These perceptions are rooted in prodigious learning and a profoundly humane sensibility.

I am happy that this remarkable man, who has searched far, who has found and reclaimed the uncluttered vision of the primitive at the crossroads of science and song, has bestowed on my country the benefit of his deep scholarly, humanistic, and spiritual meditation. *The New York Review of Books* of May 22, 1969, carried a long article, "Biafra Revisited," by Conor Cruise O'Brien on the second visit he made with Stanley Diamond. It was accompanied by a poem I had just written in memory of Christopher Okigbo, Africa's greatest modern poet, who had recently died on the Biafran battlefield. It also carried a profoundly moving poem, "Sunday in Biafra," by Stanley Diamond, which, like all his poetry, combines startling substantiality with a haunting ease and inevitability, and stamps on the mind like an icon of Africa's tragedy an image and a logic that nothing will remove.

1992

Africa Is People

I believe it was in the first weeks of 1989 that I received an invitation to an anniversary meeting—the twenty-fifth year, or something like that—of the Organisation for Economic Co-operation and Development (OECD), in Paris. I accepted without quite figuring out what I could possibly contribute to such a meeting/celebration. My initial puzzlement continued right into the meeting itself. In fact it grew as the proceedings got under way. Here was I, an African novelist among predominantly Western bankers and economists; a guest, as it were, from the world's poverty-stricken provinces at a gathering of the rich and powerful in the metropolis. As I listened to them—Europeans, Americans, Canadians, Australians—I was left in no doubt, by the assurance they displayed, that these were the masters of our world, savoring the benefits of their success. They read and discussed papers on economic and development matters in different regions of the world. They talked in particular about the magic bullet of the 1980s, structural adjustment, specially designed for those parts of the world where economies had gone completely haywire. The matter was really simple, the experts seemed to be saying: the only reason for failure to develop was indiscipline of all kinds, and the remedy a quick, sharp administration of shock treatment that would yank the sufferer out of the swamp of improvidence back onto the high and firm road of free-market economy. The most recurrent prescriptions for this condition were the removal of subsidies on food and fuel and the devaluation of the national currency. Yes, the experts conceded, some pain would inevitably accompany these measures, but such pain was transitory and, in any case, negligible in comparison to the disaster that would surely take place if nothing was done now.

Then the governor of the Bank of Kenya made his presentation. As I recall the events, he was probably the only other African at that session. He asked the experts to consider the case of Zambia, which according to him had accepted, and had been practicing, a structural adjustment regime for many years, and whose economic condition was now worse than it had been when they began their treatment. An American expert who seemed to command great attention and was accorded high deference in the room spoke again. He repeated what had already been said many times before. "Be patient, it will work, in time. Trust me"—or words to that effect.

Suddenly I received something like a stab of insight and it became clear to me why I had been invited, what I was doing there in that strange assembly. I signaled my desire to speak and was given the floor. I told them what I had just recognized. I said that what was going on before me was a *fiction workshop,* no more and no less! Here you are, spinning your fine theories, to be tried out in your imaginary laboratories. You are developing new drugs and feeding them to a bunch of laboratory guinea pigs and hoping for the best. I have news for you. Africa is not fiction. Africa is people, real people. Have you thought of that? You are brilliant people, world experts. You may even have the very best intentions. But have you thought, *really* thought, of Africa as people? I will tell you the experience of my own country, Nigeria, with structural adjustment. After two years of this remedy, we saw the country's minimum wage plummet in value from the equivalent of fifteen British pounds a month to five pounds. This is not a lab report; it is not a mathematical exercise. We are talking about someone whose income, which is already miserable enough, is now cut down to one-third of what it was two years ago. And this flesh-and-blood man has a wife and children. You say he should simply go home and tell them to be patient. Now let me ask you this question. Would you recommend a similar remedy to your own people and your own government? How do you sell such a project to an elected president? You are asking him to commit political suicide, or perhaps to get rid of elections altogether until he has fixed the economy. Do you realize that's what you are doing?

I thought I could read astonishment on some of the faces on the opposite side of the huge circular table of the conference room. Or perhaps it was just my optimistic imagination. But one thing I do know for a fact. The director-general (or whatever he was called) of the OECD, beside whom I was sitting, a Dutchman and quite a giant, had muttered to me, under his breath, at least twice: "Give it to them!"

I came away from that strange conference with enhanced optimism for the human condition. For who could have imagined that in the very heart of the enemy's citadel a friend like that Dutchman might be lurking, happy enough to set my cat among his own pigeons! "Africa is people" may seem too simple and too obvious to some of us. But I have found in the course of my travels through the world that the most simple things can still give us a lot of trouble, even the brightest among us: and this is particularly so in matters concerning Africa. One of the greatest men of the twentieth century, Albert Schweitzer—philosopher, theologian, musician, medical missionary—failed completely to see the most obvious fact about Africa and so went ahead to say: "The African is indeed my brother, but my junior brother." Now, did we or did anyone we know take Dr. Schweitzer up on that blasphemy? Oh no. On the contrary, he was admired to the point of adoration, and Lamberene, the very site on African soil where he uttered his outrage, was turned into a place of pilgrimage.

Or let us take another much admired twentieth-century figure, the first writer, as it happens, to grace the cover of the newly founded *Time* magazine. I am talking, of course, about that extraordinary Polish-born, French-speaking English sea captain and novelist, Joseph Conrad. He recorded in his memoir his first experience of seeing a black man in these remarkable words:

A certain enormous buck nigger encountered in Haiti fixed my conception of blind, furious, unreasoning rage, as manifested in the human animal to the end of my days. Of the nigger I used to dream for years afterwards.[1]

My attention was first drawn to these observations of Conrad's in a scholarly work, not very widely known, by Jonah Raskin. Its title was *The Mythology of Imperialism,* and it was published in 1971 by Random House. I mention this because Mr. Raskin's title defines the cultural source out of which Conrad derived his words and ideas. Conrad's fixation, admitted so openly by him in his memoir, and conspicuously present in his fiction, has gone largely unremarked in literary and scholarly evaluations of his work. Why? Because it is grounded quite firmly in that mythology of imperialism which has so effectively conditioned contemporary civilization and its modes of education. Imperial domination required a new language to describe the world it had created and the people it had subjugated. Not surprisingly, this new language did not celebrate these subject peoples nor toast them as heroes. Rather, it painted them in the most lurid colors. Africa, being European imperialism's prime target, with hardly a square foot escaping the fate of imperial occupation, naturally received the full measure of this adverse definition. Add to that the massive derogatory endeavor of the previous three centuries of the Atlantic slave trade to label black people, and we can begin to get some idea of the magnitude of the problem we may have today with the simple concept: *Africa is people.*

James Baldwin made an analogous point about black people in America, descendants of Africa. In his essay "Fifth Avenue, Uptown," he wrote:

Negroes want to be treated like men: a perfectly straightforward statement containing seven words. People who have mastered Kant, Hegel, Shakespeare, Marx, Freud and the Bible find this statement impenetrable.

The point of all this is to alert us to the image burden that Africa bears today and make us recognize how that image has molded contemporary attitudes, including perhaps our own, to that continent.

Do I hear in my mind's ear someone sighing wearily: "There we go again, another session of whining and complaining!"? Let me assure you that I personally abhor and detest whiners. Those who know me will already know this. To those who don't, I recommend a little pamphlet I wrote at a critical point in my country's troubles. I called it *The Trouble with Nigeria,* and it is arguably the harshest statement ever made on that unhappy country. It is so harsh that whenever I see one of the many foreign critics of Nigeria quoting gleefully from it I want to strangle him! No, I am not an apologist for Africa's many failings. And I am hardheaded enough to realize that we must not be soft on them, must never go out to justify them. But I am also rational enough to realize that we should strive to understand our failings objectively and not simply swallow the mystifications and mythologies cooked up by those whose goodwill we have every reason to suspect.

Now, I understand and accept the logic that if a country mismanages its resources it should be prepared to face the music of hard times. Long ago I wrote a novel about a young African man, well educated, full of promise and good intentions, who nevertheless got his affairs (fiscal and otherwise) in a big mess. And did he pay dearly for it!

I did not blame the banks for his inability to manage his finances. What I did do, or try to do, was offer leads to my readers for exploring the roots of the hero's predicament by separating those factors for which an individual may justly be held accountable from others that are systemic and beyond the individual's control. That critical, analytical adventure to which the book invites its readers will be medicine after death for my hero, but the reader can at least go away with the satisfaction of having tried to be fair and just to the doomed man, and the reward, hopefully, of a little enlightenment on the human condition for himself.

The countries of Africa (especially sub-Saharan Africa) on whom I am focusing my attention are not the only ones who suffer the plight of poverty in the world today. All the so-called Third World peoples are, more or less, in the same net, as indeed are all the poor everywhere, even in the midst of plenty in the First and Second Worlds.

Like the unfortunate young man in my novel, the poor of the world may be guilty of this and that particular fault or foolishness, but if we are fair we will admit that nothing they have done or left undone quite explains all the odds we see stacked up against them. We are sometimes tempted to look upon the poor as so many ne'er-do-wells we can simply ignore. But they will return to haunt our peace, because they are greater than their badge of suffering, because they are human.

I recall watching news on television about fighting in the

Horn of Africa, between Ethiopia and Eritrea. As I had come to expect, the news was very short indeed. The only background material the newscaster gave to flesh out the bald announcement of the fight was that Ethiopia and Eritrea were among the world's poorest nations. And he was off, to other news and other places, leaving me a little space and time to mull over the bad news from Africa. How much additional enlightenment did that piece of information about poverty give the viewer about the fighting or the fighters? Not much. What about telling the viewer, in the same number of words, that Eritrea was a province of Ethiopia until recently? But no. The poverty synecdoche is more attractive and less trouble; you simply reach for it from the handy storehouse of mythology about Africa. No taxing research required here.

But if poverty springs so readily to our minds when we think about Africa, how much do we really know about it?

In 1960 a bloody civil war broke out in Congo soon after its colonizer, Belgium, beat a hasty retreat from the territory. Within months its young, radical, and idealistic prime minister, Patrice Lumumba, was brutally murdered by his rivals, who replaced him with a corrupt demagogue called Mobutu, whose main attraction was presumably his claim to be an anticommunist. Mobutu set about plundering the wealth of this vast country, as large as the whole of Western Europe, and also fomenting trouble in Congo's neighboring countries, aiding and abetting the destabilization of Angola and openly cooperating with the apartheid white-minority regime in South Africa. Mobutu's legacy was truly horrendous. He stole and stashed away billions in foreign banks. He even stole his country's name and rebaptized it Zaire. Today Congo, strategically positioned in the heart of Africa, vast in size and mineral wealth, has also become one of the poorest nations on earth. Whom are we to hold responsible for this: the Congolese people, Mobutu, or his sponsors, the CIA? Who will pay the penalty of structural adjustment? Of course, that question is already irrelevant. The people are already adjusted to grinding poverty and long-range instability.

Congo is by no means the only country in Africa to have foreign powers choose or sustain its leader. It is merely the most scandalous case, in scale and effrontery.

President Clinton was right on target when he apologized to Africa for the unprincipled conduct of American foreign policy during the Cold War, a policy that scorched the young hopes of Africa's independence struggle like seedlings in a drought. I have gone into all this unpleasant matter not to prompt any new apologies but to make all of us wary of those easy, facile comments about Africa's incurable poverty or the endemic incapacity of Africans to get their act together and move ahead like everybody else.

I cannot presume to tell world bankers anything about public finance or economics and the rest. I have told you stories. Now let me make a couple of suggestions.

In the late 1990s an organization in Britain called Jubilee 2000 informed me of their noble campaign to persuade leaders of the world's rich nations (the G8 countries) to forgive the debts owed them by the world's fifty poorest nations. I was made to understand that the British government was half persuaded that it should be done, and that the Canadians were possibly of the same view. But, on the negative side, I learned that Japan and Germany were adamantly opposed to the proposal. About the most important factor, America, my informant had this to say: "When asked about cancellation their tongues speak sweetly, like some of Homer's Greeks, but their hearts are closed. It needs another poet to go to them and lay siege to those hearts . . . will you be that poet?" Subsequently, my wife, noticing perhaps my anxiety, showed me a passage in a book she happened to be reading. "The fact that a message may not be received is no reason not to send it." I was startled by the message and the mystery of its timely surfacing. I also recognized the affinity between this thought and another I knew, wearing its proverbial Igbo dress: "Let us perform the sacrifice and leave the blame on the doorstep of the spirits." That's what I have now done.

Regarding Japan and Germany, beneficiaries both of postwar reconstruction assistance, I did not appeal to their hearts but instead nudged their memories and their sense of irony. And for good measure I told them the parable of Jesus about the servant who was forgiven a huge debt by his master, on leaving whose audience he chanced upon a fellow servant who owed him a very small sum of money. The first servant seized him by the throat and had him tortured and thrown into prison.

My second request to the World Bank went to the very root of the problem—the looting of the wealth of poor nations by corrupt leaders and their cronies. This crime is compounded by the expatriation of these funds into foreign banks, where they are put into the service of foreign economies. Consequently the victim country is defrauded twice, if my economics is correct: it is defrauded of the wealth which is stolen from its treasury and also of the development potential of that wealth forever.

In asking the World Bank to take a lead in the recovery of the stolen resources of poor countries, I did not suggest that such criminal transactions are made through the World Bank. I am also aware that banks are not set up normally to act as a police force. But we live in terrible times when an individual tyrant or a small clique of looters in power can destroy the lives and the future of whole countries and whole populations by their greed. The consequences of these actions can be of truly genocidal proportions.

Herein lies the root of the horrifying statistic to which the president of the World Bank, James Wolfensohn, drew attention: "You will be staggered to know, as I was, that 37 percent of African private wealth is held outside Africa, whereas for Asia the share is 3 percent and for Latin America it is 17 percent."[2]

It would be a great pity, I remarked, if the world were to sit back in the face of these catastrophic statistics and do nothing, merely to preserve codes of banking etiquette and confidentiality formulated for quite other times. The world woke up too late to the inadequacy of these codes in the matter of the Nazi Holocaust gold. We had thus been warned. The cooperation of the world's banks, led by the World Bank Group, in eliminating this great scourge would have given so many poor countries the first real opportunity to begin afresh and take responsibility for their development and progress, and it would have discouraged future marauders of nations. It would also have cleared the world's banking systems of the charges of receiving stolen property and colluding with genocide.

For too long the world has been content to judge peoples and nations in distress largely on the basis of received stereotypes drawn from mythologies of oppression. In 1910, at the height of British imperial dominion, John Buchan, a popular novelist who was also a distinguished imperial civil servant, published a colonialist classic entitled *Prester John,* in which we find the following pronouncement: "That is the difference between white and black, the gift of responsibility."

I do not believe such a difference exists, except in the mythology of domination. Let's put this to the test by giving these poor, black nations the first sporting chance of their lives. The cost is low and the rewards will blow our minds, white and black alike. Trust me!

Let me round this up with a nice little coda. "Africa is people" has another dimension. Africa believes in people, in cooperation with people. If the philosophical dictum of Descartes "I think, therefore I am" represents a European individualistic ideal, the Bantu declaration *"Umuntu ngumuntu ngabantu"* represents an African communal aspiration: "A human is human because of other humans."

Our humanity is contingent on the humanity of our fellows. No person or group can be human alone. We rise above the animal together, or not at all. If we learned that lesson even this late in the day, we would have taken a truly millennial step forward.

1998

Notes

The Education of a British-Protected Child

1. Guy Burrows, *The Land of the Pigmies* (London: 1898), quoted in Robert Kimbrough's edition of Joseph Conrad's *Heart of Darkness* (New York: Norton, 1988), pp. 128, 130.
2. Robert B. Shepard, *Nigeria, Africa and the United States* (Bloomington and Indianapolis: Indiana University Press, 1991), pp. 88, 89.

Spelling Our Proper Name

1. James Baldwin, "My Dungeon Shook: Letter to My Nephew on the One Hundredth Anniversary of the Emancipation," *The Fire Next Time,* 1963.
2. John Buchan, *Prester John,* quoted in Brian V. Street: *The Savage in Literature* (London, Boston: Routledge & K Paul, 1975), p. 14.
3. James Baldwin, "My Dungeon Shook: Letter to My Nephew on the One Hundredth Anniversary of the Emancipation," *The Fire Next Time,* 1963.
4. Basil Davidson, *The African Slave Trade* (Boston: Atlantic–Little, Brown, 1961), pp. 147–148. Quoted in Chinweizu, *The West and the Rest of Us* (Pero Press, 1987), p. 28.
5. C. R. Boxer, "The Kingdom of Congo," *The Dawn of African History,* Roland Oliver, ed. (London: Oxford University Press, 1968), p. 78. Quoted in Chinweizu, *The West and the Rest of Us,* p. 331.

6. Dorothy Randall Tsuruta, "James Baldwin and Chinua Achebe," *Black Scholar,* no. 12 (March–April 1981), p. 73.

Recognitions

1. *The Interesting Narrative of the Life of Olaudah Equiano, or Gustavus Vassa, the African. Written by Himself,* edited and with an introduction by Paul Edwards (Harlow and White Plains, N.Y.: Longman, 1989).

Africa's Tarnished Name

1. Dorothy Hammond and Alta Jablow, *The Africa That Never Was: Four Centuries of British Writing about Africa* (Prospect Heights, Ill.: Waveland Press, 1992), pp. 22–23.
2. Joseph Conrad, *Heart of Darkness,* ed. Robert Kimbrough (New York: Norton, 1972), p. 37.
3. Ibid.
4. Ibid., p. 4.
5. I am indebted to Basil Davidson's *The African Slave Trade* (Boston: Little, Brown and Company, 1980) for the outline of this story.
6. Mbanza was the capital of the kingdom of Congo; the king soon renamed it São Salvador. The quoted passage is from Davidson, *The African Slave Trade,* p. 136.
7. Ibid., p. 152.
8. Joseph Conrad. "Geography and Some Explorers," *National Geographic* (March 1924).
9. Davidson, *The African Slave Trade,* p. 147.
10. Sylvia Leith-Ross, *African Women: A Study of the Igbo of Nigeria* (London: Faber and Faber, 1938); see p. 19.
11. Conrad, *Heart of Darkness,* pp. 38–39.
12. Ibid., p. 51.
13. Davidson, op. cit., p. 29.
14. Conrad, *Heart of Darkness,* p. 147.
15. David Livingstone, *Missionary Travels,* quoted in Hammond and Jablow, *The Africa That Never Was,* p. 43.

16. Reyahn King et al., *Ignatius Sancho: An African Man of Letters* (London: National Portrait Gallery, 1997), p. 28.
17. Ibid., p. 30.
18. William F. Schultz and Willis Hartshorn, "1997 Amnesty International Calendar: Photographs from the Collection of the International Center of Photography" (New York: Universe Publishing, 1996).
19. Ibid.

Politics and Politicians of Language in African Literature

1. Obiajunwa Wali. "The Dead End of African Literature?" *Transition* 4, no. 10 (September 10, 1963).
2. Ngũgĩ wa Thiong'o. "The Language of African Literature," *Decolonising the Mind: The Politics of Language in African Literature* (London: Heinemann, 1986).
3. Ibid.
4. Richard Symonds, *The British and Their Successors* (Evanston, Ill.: Northwestern University Press, 1966), p. 202.
5. David R. Smock and Kwamena Bentsi-Enchill, eds., *The Search for National Integration in Africa* (London: Collier Macmillan, 1975), p. 174.
6. J. F. Ade Ajay, *Christian Missions in Nigeria, 1841–1891* (London, 1965), pp. 133–34.
7. Smock and Enchill, *The Search for National Integration in Africa,* p. 176.

African Literature as Restoration of Celebration

1. Quoted in Brian Street, *The Savage in Literature* (London and Boston: Routledge and Kegan Paul, 1975), p. 14.
2. Philip D. Curtin, *The Image of Africa: British Ideas and Actions* (Madison: University of Wisconsin Press, 1964), p. vi.
3. Conrad, *Heart of Darkness,* p. 37.
4. Cheikh Hamidou Kane, *Ambiguous Adventure,* Katherine Woods, trans. (London: Heinemann, 1972), p. 37.
5. Ibid., p. 79.

Teaching *Things Fall Apart*

1. From "In Dialogue to Define Aesthetics: James Baldwin and Chinua Achebe," *The Black Scholar* 12 (March–April 1981), *Conversations with James Baldwin.*
2. Jules Chametzky, *Our Decentralized Literature* (Amherst: University of Massachusetts Press, 1986).

Martin Luther King and Africa

1. Davidson, *The African Slave Trade,* p. 12.
2. Ibid., p. 25.
3. Dorothy Randall Tsuruta, "In Dialogue to Define Aesthetics: James Baldwin and Chinua Achebe," *The Black Scholar* 12 (March–April 1981), p. 73.

Stanley Diamond

1. House of Lords Official Report, August 27, 1968.
2. Suzanne Cronje, *The World and Nigeria: The Diplomatic History of the Biafran War, 1967–1970* (London: Sidgwick & Jackson, 1972), p. 211.

Africa Is People

1. Quoted in Jonah Raskin, *The Mythology of Imperialism* (New York: Random House, 1971).
2. James D. Wolfensohn, *Africa's Moment* (Washington, D.C.: The World Bank, 1998).

Acknowledgments

Some of the essays in this work originally appeared, sometimes in slightly different form, as follows:

"The Education of a British-Protected Child": Adapted from a speech delivered as the Ashby Lecture, Cambridge University, January 22, 1993.

"The Sweet Aroma of Zik's Kitchen: Growing Up in the Ambience of a Legend": Adapted from a speech delivered at Lincoln University in Pennsylvania, April 1994. This speech was given at a conference honoring Dr. Nnamdi Azikiwe, hosted and sponsored by Lincoln University's president, Niara Sudarkasa.

"My Dad and Me": From *My Dad and Me: A Heartwarming Collection of Stories About Fathers from a Host of Larry's Famous Friends.* Larry King (New York: Crown, 1996).

"What is Nigeria to Me?": Adapted from the keynote address at *The Guardian*'s Silver Jubilee, at the Nigerian Institute of International Affairs (NIIA), Victoria Island, Lagos, on October 9, 2008. It was subsequently reprinted in the *Nigeria Daily News* on October 14, 2008.

"Traveling White": Originally published in *The Weekend Guardian* (London), October 22, 1989.

"Spelling Our Proper Name": Adapted from a speech delivered at a conference entitled "Black Writers Redefine the Struggle," on the occasion of the death of James Baldwin, at the University of Massachusetts at Amherst, April 22-23, 1988. It was subsequently published in an earlier form in

A Tribute to James Baldwin (Amherst: University of Massachusetts Press, 1989).

"Africa's Tarnished Name": Originally published in *Another Africa*. Robert Lyons and Chinua Achebe (Anchor Books, 1998).

"Politics and Politicians of Language in African Literature": Originally published as "Politics and Politicians of Language in African Literature" in *FILLM* (International Federation for Modern Languages and Literatures) *Proceedings*. Ed. Doug Killam (Guelph, Ontario: University of Guelph, 1989).

"African Literature as Restoration of Celebration": From *Chinua Achebe: A Celebration*. Eds. Kirsten Holst Petersen and Anna Rutherford (Oxford and Portsmouth, NH: Heinemann; Sydney, Australia and Coventry, England: Dangeroo Press, 1990), 1-10.

"Teaching *Things Fall Apart*": From *Approaches to Teaching Achebe's* Things Fall Apart. Ed. Bernth Lindfors. Approaches to Teaching World Literature Series: 37 (New York: Modern Language Association, 1991), 20-24. Reprinted in *Morning Yet on Creation Day*.

"Martin Luther King and Africa": Originated as a talk given at the King Holiday Celebration, January 20, 1992, at the Smithsonian Institution National Museum of History in Washington, D.C.

"The University and the Leadership Factor in Nigerian Politics": From *The University and the Leadership Factor in Nigerian Politics* (Enugu, Nigeria: ABIC Books and Equipment, 1988).

"Stanley Diamond": From *Dialectical Anthropology: Essays in Honor of Stanley Diamond: The Politics of Culture and Creativity*. Ed. Christine Ward Gailey (University of Florida Press, May 1992).

"Africa Is People": Adapted from a speech originally delivered at the Organisation for Economic Co-operation and Development in Paris, France, 1998. Subsequently published in *Massachusetts Review* 40.3 (Autumn 1999).